ANNE WILLAN'S
LOOK&COOK

Classic Breads

ANNE WILLAN'S
LOOK&COOK

Classic Breads

Stoddart

A DORLING KINDERSLEY BOOK

Created and produced by
CARROLL & BROWN LIMITED
5 Lonsdale Road
London NW6 6RA

Project Editor Valerie Cipollone
Assistant Editors Stella Vayne and Anne Crane

Editorial Consultant Jeni Wright

Art Editor Susan Knight
Designers Alan Watt and Lucy De Rosa

Photographers David Murray and Jules Selmes

Production Wendy Rogers and Amanda Mackie

First published in Canada in 1995
by Stoddart Publishing Co., Limited
34 Lesmill Road, Toronto, Canada M3B 2T6

Canadian Cataloguing-in-Publication Data

Willan, Anne.
Classic breads.
(Anne Willan's Look and cook).
Includes index.
ISBN 0-7737-2855-4
1. Cookery (Bread). I. Title. II. Series: Willan, Anne.
Anne Willan's Look & cook.

TX769.W55 1995   641.8'15   C94-932851-0

Reproduced by Colourscan, Singapore
Printed and bound in Italy by A. Mondadori, Verona

CONTENTS

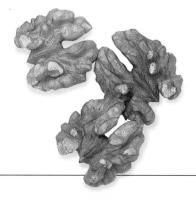

CLASSIC BREADS

THE LOOK & COOK APPROACH

Welcome to **Classic Breads** and the *Look & Cook* series. These volumes are designed to be the simplest, most informative cookbooks you will ever own. They are the closest I can come to sharing my personal techniques for making my own favorite recipes without actually being with you in the kitchen looking over your shoulder.

EQUIPMENT

Equipment and ingredients often determine whether or not you can make a particular recipe, so *Look & Cook* illustrates everything you need at the beginning of each one. You will see at a glance how long a recipe takes to bake, how many loaves it makes, what the finished bread looks like, and

---
INGREDIENTS

how much preparation can be done ahead. When you start, you will find the preparation and baking organized into steps that are easy to follow. Each stage has its own color coding and everything is shown in photographs with brief text accompanying each step. You will never be in doubt as to what it is you are doing, why you are doing it, and how it should look.

🍽 MAKES 12 🥄 WORK TIME 20–25 MINUTES ♨ BAKING TIME 15–20 MINUTES

I have also included helpful hints and ideas under "Anne Says." These may list an alternative ingredient or piece of equipment, or explain a certain method, or offer some advice on mastering a particular technique. Similarly, if there is a crucial stage in a recipe when things can go astray, I have included some warnings called "Take Care."

Many of the photographs are annotated to pinpoint why certain pieces of equipment work best, and how bread dough should look at the various stages of preparation. Because presentation is so important, a picture of the finished bread with serving suggestions is at the end of each recipe.

Thanks to all this information, you cannot go wrong. I will be with you every step of the way. So please come with me into the kitchen to look, cook, and enjoy some delicious **Classic Breads.**

WHY BREADS?

If you were to study cuisines from around the world, it would be difficult to find any ritual more celebrated than the long-practiced science and art of bread baking. No facet of our culinary repertoire is as rich with history as the harvesting of grain and the baking of bread. Bread is baked in infinite variety, and these are just a few of my favorite recipes.

RECIPE CHOICE

Breads are easily divided into two categories: those raised with yeast and those made with chemical leaveners. Here I will show you a variety of yeast breads, plain and fancy, ranging from a basic white loaf to festive breads enriched with eggs and butter. You will also learn how to bake quick breads. As their name implies, these cake-like breads are fast and easy to prepare because the yeast is replaced with baking powder, baking soda, or a combination of the two.

BASIC YEAST BREADS

Split-Top White Bread: this white bread is enriched with milk, then slashed down the center to split during baking. An indispensable recipe for novice and veteran bakers alike. *Cinnamon Swirl Bread:* perfect for the breakfast table, white bread is enriched with butter and spiced with a mixture of cinnamon and sugar. *Whole Wheat Bread:* honey sweetens a dough made of stone-ground whole wheat. It is shaped into two-tiered cottage loaves. *Double Wheat Bread:* bulghur wheat enhances the flavor of this bread. It is baked in clay pots. *Sourdough Bread:* sourdough starter ferments for 3–5 days in order to develop its characteristic sour flavor, so plan ahead to enjoy these crusty, slightly tangy loaves. *Sourdough Rolls:* the same sourdough is shaped into individual rolls. Great for picnic lunches. *Multi-Grain Breakfast Bread:* for this hearty bread, buttermilk softens a combination of whole wheat and white flours fortified with rolled oats, wheat bran, cornmeal, and toasted sunflower seeds. *Orange Juice Breakfast Bread:* orange juice flavors this multi-grain loaf snipped for a hedgehog finish. *French Baguette:* the dough for these traditional stick-shaped loaves is left to rise three times, developing a chewy, honeycombed crumb, and a full flavor. The crust bakes to a crisp golden brown. *Wheat Ear Baguette (Epi):* baguette loaves are snipped deeply just before baking to resemble ears of wheat. *Seeded Rye Bread:* caraway seeds and rye are a classic combination. The dough

makes a dark, crusty loaf calling for delicatessen sandwiches and a side of slaw. *Horseshoe Rye Bread:* rye stands alone in this variation, shaped into a large horseshoe.

SPECIALTY YEAST BREADS

Dinner Rolls: this egg-enriched dough is easy to twist and roll into a choice of 6 decorative shapes. *Challah:* for this traditional Jewish bread, made for the Sabbath, holidays, and other festive occasions, four strands of dough are braided, glazed with egg yolk, and sprinkled with poppy seeds – delicious any time. *Kugelhopf with Walnuts, Bacon, and Herbs:* this tender bread from Alsace is flavored with diced bacon, fresh herbs, and chopped walnuts, and is baked in a traditional fluted mold. *Kugelhopf with Raisins and Almonds:* a dusting of confectioners' sugar hints at the sweet filling of raisins and chopped almonds in this cake-like bread. *Onion and Walnut Crown:* sautéed onion and toasted walnuts add rich flavor to basic white bread. The dough is shaped into a ring, then the top is snipped to fashion a giant crown. *Green and Black Olive Bread:* pungent oil-cured olives, a flavor redolent of Provence, are kneaded into the dough for this rustic bread. *Small Brioches:* eggs and butter give this classic French bread its rich flavor and crumb. Each roll is topped with a "head" and baked in a scalloped mold. *Rich Brioche:* kneading in additional butter makes this dough extra rich. The brioche dough is baked in two large molds. *Cheese Brioche:* Brie cheese replaces some of the butter in this bread. Rounds of dough are dropped into a loaf pan for a decorative loaf. *Potato-Chive Monkey Bread:* mashed potato makes a loaf with a moist and tender crumb. The chive-studded dough is rolled into small balls, then arranged and baked in a ring mold. An American favorite. *Sour Cream and Dill Bread:* sour cream and dill flavor this hearty potato bread.

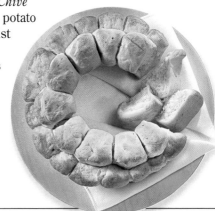

Sesame Breadsticks (Grissini Siciliani): thin and crisp, these breadsticks are a great addition to the antipasto table. *Spanish Bread Loops (Picos):* the same dough is made into miniature loaves and sprinkled with coarse sea salt. *Pesto Garland Bread:* a ring of dough is sliced and fanned to reveal swirls of pesto. *Sun-dried Tomato Spiral:* a gutsy filling of sun-dried tomatoes, garlic, basil, and Parmesan is wrapped within a spiral of dough. *Spiced Lamb Pies:* a Middle Eastern favorite, flat bread makes a tender shell for a ground lamb filling spiced with garlic, ginger, cumin, and fresh and ground coriander (cilantro). *Pita Bread:* classic Middle Eastern pocket bread is flecked with cumin seeds and baked in a very hot oven until it puffs. *Cornmeal Pizzas with Onion Confit and Gorgonzola:* red onions made sweet by slow cooking and pungent Gorgonzola cheese work well together on these crisp-crusted individual cornmeal pizzas. *Cornmeal Pizzas with Ricotta and Spinach:* in the spirit of the red, white, and green, sliced plum tomatoes top ricotta cheese and sautéed spinach. Buon appetito! *Chicago Deep-Dish Pizza:* famous for its thick crust, this pizza is made with fresh tomato sauce, mild Italian sausage, and mozzarella cheese. *Pizza Calabrese:* flavors of the Mediterranean – capers, black olives, and artichoke hearts – feature in these stuffed pizzas. *Focaccia with Rosemary:* olive oil is key in this spongy Italian flat bread, and rosemary is a classic flavoring. *Focaccia with Sage:* when slashed, this sage-speckled dough bakes to resemble a leaf. *Chocolate Bread:* unsweetened cocoa powder colors this richly flavored loaf studded with chunks of bittersweet chocolate. *Chocolate and Orange Rolls:* grated orange zest replaces the cocoa powder, and the dough is shaped into giant rolls. *Aunt Louie's Yule Bread:* tea-soaked dried currants and golden raisins, and candied orange peel are added to a richly spiced dough perfect for the winter holidays. *Yorkshire Yule Bread:* this bread is spiked with a generous tot of whiskey, and baked in a charlotte mold.

QUICK BREADS

Old-Fashioned Cornbread: a cast-iron skillet gives a crisp golden crust to cornbread studded with whole kernels of fresh corn. *Corn Muffins with Roasted Bell Pepper:* roasted red bell pepper sweetens cornbread batter baked in a muffin tin. *Irish Soda Bread:* a simple bread of stone-ground whole wheat flour and buttermilk leavened with baking soda. *Griddle Cakes:* with the addition of rolled oats and a little more buttermilk, the dough for Irish Soda Bread turns into a batter for cakes cooked on a hot griddle. Delicious with butter and homemade jam. *Skillet Bread:* here, a combination of stone-ground and all-purpose flours is used, the dough is cut into wedges, and cooked to golden brown in a skillet. *Southern Buttermilk Biscuits:* a light hand is the trick to making these down-home favorites, equally good with a sweet or savory accompaniment. *Chive Drop Biscuits:* when the quantity of buttermilk is increased, biscuit dough softens and can be dropped from a spoon onto the baking sheet. Drop biscuits are especially delicious when made with fresh chives. *Currant Scones:* the same biscuit dough doubles for scones when studded with dried currants and cut into wedges. *Orange-Zucchini Bread:* freshly grated zucchini keeps this spiced bread moist. The zucchini skin is left on to add specks of color to the batter, and chopped walnuts add a crunchy texture. *Pumpkin Bread:* pumpkin and spice are a natural combination – great for warming up chilly days. *Banana Bread:* mashed bananas, the riper the better, are a sweet addition to this quick bread baked in miniature loaf pans. Try it spread with cream cheese. *Lemon-Blueberry Muffins:* lots of fresh blueberries and grated lemon zest make these muffins delicious. For extra lemon flavor, they are glazed with lemon juice and sugar. *Lemon-Poppy Seed Muffins:* poppy seeds add flavor and crunch to muffins flavored with both lemon juice and zest. Sugar is sprinkled on top before baking for a sweet, crispy finish.

EQUIPMENT

Getting your hands wet, as it were, is the beauty of bread making. And as luck would have it, for yeast doughs, your hands are by far the most useful kitchen tool. When mixing and kneading, their warmth helps to activate the yeast even before the dough is left to rise. They are the gauge with which to measure the condition of the dough, helping you judge its progress by how it feels.

A generous work surface for kneading the dough is important, whether made of Formica, wood, or stainless steel. It should be the right height for your extended hands to reach the surface comfortably so you can knead dough forcefully without straining your back. When making and letting dough rise, a selection of glass, ceramic, or stainless steel bowls is needed, while a pastry scraper comes in handy for doughs made directly on the work surface.

The final step before baking some loaves is slashing the tops to make ornamental designs. A sharp edge is vital to cut the dough without dragging – a utility knife or single-edged razor blade works well. A very sharp small knife or chef's knife can also be used, depending on the size of the job at hand. A pair of pointed kitchen scissors can come in handy for snipping the dough, too.

Flat breads and rolls are at their best hot from the oven, but most loaves are best left to cool before slicing. A wire rack allows air to circulate as the bread cools, as well as speeding cooling time and helping a crisp crust to stay that way. A serrated bread knife cuts the neatest slices.

You will need a chef's knife for dividing raw dough and chopping nuts and vegetables, as well as a chopping board, vegetable peeler, grater, and citrus juicer. Other standard kitchen equipment used for bread making includes a pastry brush for buttering and oiling bowls and glazing unbaked loaves, a rubber spatula for mixing quick bread batter, and a strainer for sifting dry ingredients. Saucepans and frying pans are used to heat liquids and prepare several of the fillings.

SPECIALTY MOLDS

There are countless possibilities for varying the shape and size of a loaf of bread, some of which require specialized equipment. A number of breads are shaped in molds such as a miniature, medium, or large loaf pan, a muffin tin, a soufflé dish, or even a clay flower pot. Specialty molds include small scalloped molds for Small Brioches, and larger scalloped

molds for Rich Brioche, a bucket-shaped charlotte mold for Yorkshire Yule Bread, a fluted kugelhopf mold for Kugelhopf with Raisins and Almonds, a baguette frame for French Baguette, a ring mold for Potato-Chive Monkey Bread, a jelly roll pan for Focaccia with Rosemary, a cast-iron skillet for Old-Fashioned Cornbread and Skillet Bread, and a deep-dish pizza pan for Chicago Deep-Dish Pizza. For free-form loaves and pizzas, baking sheets are essential. Wherever possible, substitutions for specialty molds are given – for instance, instead of using a ring mold to bake Potato-Chive Monkey Bread, a round cake pan and ramekin can also be used. In the case of Kugelhopf with Walnuts, Bacon, and Herbs, a bundt pan can be used in place of the traditional kugelhopf mold, but it does not produce a bread as nicely shaped.

MACHINES AND BREADS

Yeast doughs can be mixed and kneaded in just a few minutes with the help of a heavy-duty electric mixer fitted with paddle and dough hook attachments, or a food processor. It is important to use a stationary mixer with a fixed bowl as mixing and kneading some doughs is quite strenuous work, and can strain the motors of less powerful models. First, the paddle attachment is used to combine the liquid ingredients. Once the flour is added, the dough hook is put in place for kneading. As far as food processors are concerned, those fitted with a steel blade are suitable for kneading doughs made with small quantities of flour, while a plastic dough blade should be used for those doughs made with large quantities of flour. The use of these machines is explained in detailed "how-to" boxes.

The newest bread-making appliance is the bread machine, which makes, kneads, and bakes bread dough for you. More advanced machines even have a timer so you can wake up to the aroma of freshly baked bread. To give the loaf a more personal touch, you can take the dough out of the machine after kneading, then shape it as you like and bake it in your regular oven. Some of the recipes in this volume can be adapted for preparation in the bread machine; be sure to follow the manufacturer's instructions.

SPLIT-TOP WHITE BREAD

 MAKES 2 MEDIUM LOAVES   WORK TIME 40–50 MINUTES*   BAKING TIME 35–40 MINUTES

EQUIPMENT

saucepan

chef's knife

utility knife†

pastry brush

bowls

dish towels

two 8-x-4-x-2-inch
loaf pans

wire rack

†small knife can also be used

ANNE SAYS
"You can make and knead the dough in a heavy-duty electric mixer fitted with a dough hook."

INGREDIENTS

unbleached
all-purpose flour

milk

butter

active dry yeast

This basic white bread, a staple recipe for novice and practiced bakers alike, is made with all-purpose flour, milk, and a yeast and flour sponge – a fermented batter that adds characteristic flavor and improves the texture of plain yeast-risen breads. The finished loaves are rich in flavor, and have an even, tender crumb.

GETTING AHEAD

White loaves are best the day of baking, but can be tightly wrapped and kept for 1–2 days, or they can be frozen. The dough can also be made, kneaded, and left in the refrigerator to rise overnight. Shape the loaves, let them come to room temperature, then bake as directed.

*plus 30–60 minutes fermenting time for the sponge and 1 3/4–2 1/4 hours rising time

SHOPPING LIST

2 cups	milk, more for glaze
6 cups	unbleached all-purpose flour, more if needed
1 tbsp	salt
	butter for bowl and loaf pans
	For the sponge
2 1/2 tsp	active dry yeast, or 1/2 oz compressed yeast
1 cup	lukewarm water
1 cup	unbleached all-purpose flour, more for sprinkling

ORDER OF WORK

1 PREPARE THE SPONGE AND MAKE THE DOUGH

2 KNEAD AND LET THE DOUGH RISE

3 SHAPE THE LOAVES

4 GLAZE AND BAKE THE LOAVES

1 PREPARE THE SPONGE AND MAKE THE DOUGH

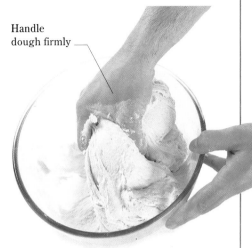

Handle dough firmly

1 Prepare the sponge (see box, below). Meanwhile, bring the milk just to a boil, and let cool to lukewarm. Once the sponge has risen, add the milk and mix with your hand.

2 Stir in half of the flour, and the salt, and mix well with your hand. Add the remaining flour, 1 cup at a time, mixing well after each addition.

3 Keep adding flour until the dough pulls away from the side of the bowl in a ball. It should be soft and slightly sticky.

HOW TO MAKE A SPONGE

The flavor and texture of bread, particularly plain loaves, is improved when the yeast first ferments in a sponge – a soft batter which froths and bubbles when the yeast starts to grow. The sponge is then mixed with the remaining ingredients to form a dough. The slower the sponge ferments, the more flavor it will have.

1 In a small bowl, sprinkle or crumble the yeast over ¹/₄ cup of the water. Let stand until dissolved, stirring once, about 5 minutes.

2 Put the dissolved yeast and remaining water into a large bowl. Stir in the flour and mix vigorously with your hand, 30–60 seconds.

3 Sprinkle the sponge with about 2 tbsp flour, covering most but not all of the surface.

4 Cover the bowl with a damp dish towel and let the sponge ferment in a warm place until the bubbles break through the flour, 30–60 minutes. Use the sponge as directed in the recipe.

2 KNEAD AND LET THE DOUGH RISE

Kneading develops gluten, helping dough to rise

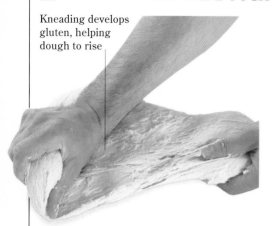

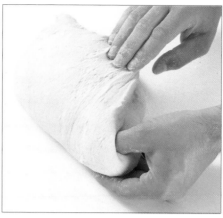

1 Turn the dough onto a floured work surface. Sprinkle the dough and your hands with flour, and begin to knead by holding the dough with one hand and pushing it away from you with the other.

2 Continue to knead by peeling the dough from the surface. Give the dough a quarter turn, and knead until it is very smooth, elastic, and forms a ball, 8–10 minutes. If the dough sticks while kneading, flour the work surface.

3 Wash the large bowl and brush it with melted butter. Put the kneaded dough in the bowl, and flip it so the surface is lightly buttered. Cover the bowl with a damp dish towel and let the dough rise in a warm place until doubled in bulk, 1–1 1/2 hours.

3 SHAPE THE LOAVES

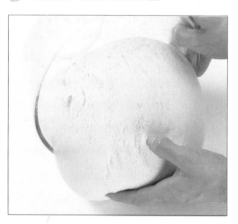

1 Brush the loaf pans with melted butter. Turn the dough onto a lightly floured work surface and knead with your hand just to knock out the air, 15–20 seconds. Cover the dough, and let rest, about 5 minutes.

2 Cut the dough in half. Cover 1 piece while shaping the other. Flour your hands and pat 1 piece of the dough into a 10- x 8-inch rectangle.

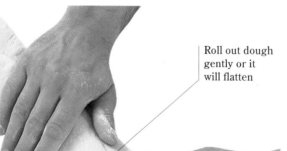

Roll out dough gently or it will flatten

3 Starting with a long side, roll the rectangle into a cylinder, pinching and sealing it with your fingers as you go. Roll the cylinder until it is about 16 inches long. With the cylinder seam-side up, fold the ends over, making it the length of the pan.

4 Drop the loaf, seam-side down, into 1 of the prepared pans. Repeat to shape the remaining dough. Cover the pans with a dry dish towel, and let the loaves rise in a warm place until the pans are just full, about 45 minutes.

4 GLAZE AND BAKE THE LOAVES

Use very sharp edge to slash

1 Heat the oven to 425°F. Brush the loaves with milk. With the utility knife, make a slash, about ½-inch deep, down the center of each loaf.

2 Bake the loaves in the heated oven, 20 minutes. Lower the heat to 375°F and continue baking until well browned, 15–20 minutes longer. Remove the loaves from the pans. Turn them over and tap the bottoms with your knuckles. The bread should sound hollow and the sides should feel crisp when pressed. Let the loaves cool completely.

🍴 TO SERVE

Serve the bread sliced and spread with butter. A full-flavored white loaf makes satisfying sandwiches.

VARIATION
CINNAMON SWIRL BREAD

When plain white dough is rolled with cinnamon and sugar, each slice reveals a dark swirl of spice.

1 Make, knead, and let the dough rise as directed in the main recipe. Brush 2 loaf pans with melted butter. In a small bowl, combine 1 tbsp ground cinnamon with ½ cup sugar. Set 2 tsp of the mixture aside for the glaze. Melt 3 tbsp unsalted butter in a small saucepan and let cool.
2 Knock the air out of the dough, and let rest as directed. Cut the dough in half, and cover 1 piece while shaping the other.
3 With a rolling pin, roll the dough into a 12- x 8-inch rectangle. Brush the rectangle with some of the melted butter, and sprinkle with half of the cinnamon and sugar mixture. Starting with a short end, roll the rectangle into a cylinder and pinch the seam and ends to seal them. Drop the loaf, seam-side down, into 1 of the prepared pans. Repeat to shape the remaining dough.
4 Cover the loaves, and let rise as directed. Do not let the loaves rise longer than directed, or the cinnamon swirl may separate.
5 Heat the oven to 425°F. Brush each loaf with more melted butter, sprinkle with the remaining cinnamon and sugar, and bake as directed. Unmold the loaves and let cool slightly. Serve the bread warm or toasted.

WHOLE WHEAT BREAD

EQUIPMENT

bowls

chef's knife

pastry brush

dish towels

wire rack

small saucepan

baking sheet

The finest whole wheat bread is made with a high proportion of stone-ground flour. Stone-ground whole wheat flour varies from mill to mill and batch to batch so you will want to experiment with this recipe, using various flours and adding more or less water. Following English tradition, I like to shape whole wheat dough into round cottage loaves. Other two-tiered loaves, oblong in shape, were once known in London as "cottage bricks."

GETTING AHEAD
Whole Wheat Bread is best the day of baking, but can be tightly wrapped and kept for 2–3 days, or it can be frozen.
*plus 1³/₄–2¹/₄ hours rising time

INGREDIENTS

stone-ground whole wheat flour

unbleached all-purpose flour

honey

unsalted butter

active dry yeast

ORDER OF WORK

1 MAKE, KNEAD, AND LET THE DOUGH RISE

2 SHAPE AND BAKE THE LOAVES

ANNE SAYS
"You can make and knead the dough in a heavy-duty electric mixer fitted with a dough hook. Instead of making cottage loaves, you can bake the dough in two 9-x5-x3-inch loaf pans."

SHOPPING LIST

¹/₄ cup	unsalted butter, more for bowl and baking sheet
3 tbsp	honey
2 cups	lukewarm water
1 tbsp	active dry yeast, or ²/₃ oz compressed yeast
1 tbsp	salt
1 cup	unbleached all-purpose flour, more if needed
5 cups	stone-ground whole wheat flour

1 MAKE, KNEAD, AND LET THE DOUGH RISE

1 Melt the butter in the saucepan. Stir 1 tbsp of the honey and ¼ cup of the water in a small bowl until mixed.

2 Sprinkle or crumble the yeast over the honey and water and let stand until dissolved, stirring once, about 5 minutes.

3 Put the melted butter, remaining honey and water, dissolved yeast, and salt into a large bowl. Stir in the all-purpose flour with half of the whole wheat flour and mix with your hand.

4 Add the remaining whole wheat flour, 1 cup at a time, mixing well after each addition. Keep adding whole wheat flour until the dough pulls away from the side of the bowl in a ball. It should be soft and slightly sticky.

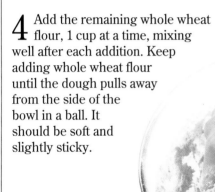

Hand is best tool for mixing in flour

Dough stiffens as flour is absorbed

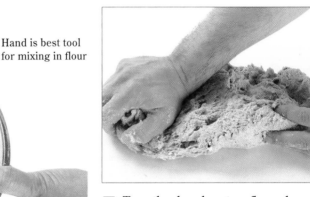

5 Turn the dough onto a floured work surface. Sprinkle it with all-purpose flour, and begin to knead by holding the dough with one hand and pushing it away from you with the other.

6 Continue to knead by peeling the dough from the surface. Give the dough a quarter turn, and knead until it is very smooth, elastic, and forms a ball, 8–10 minutes. If the dough sticks while kneading, flour the work surface.

7 Wash the large bowl and brush it with melted butter. Put the kneaded dough in the bowl, and flip it so the surface is lightly buttered. Cover the bowl with a damp dish towel and let the dough rise in a warm place until doubled in bulk, 1–1½ hours.

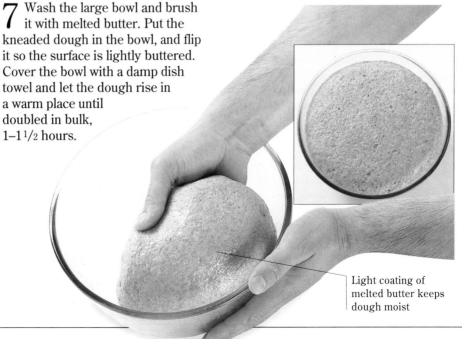

Light coating of melted butter keeps dough moist

2 SHAPE AND BAKE THE LOAVES

1 Once the dough has doubled in bulk, brush the baking sheet with melted butter.

2 Turn the dough onto a lightly floured work surface and knead with your hand just to knock out the air, 15–20 seconds. Cover the dough, and let rest, about 5 minutes.

3 With the chef's knife, cut the dough into 3 equal pieces. Cut 1 piece in half. Cover 1 large and 1 small piece of dough with a dish towel while shaping the rest.

Cut straight down through dough to prevent it sticking to knife

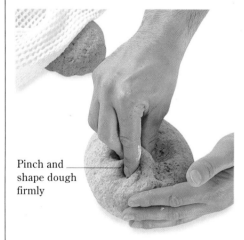

Pinch and shape dough firmly

4 Shape 1 large piece of dough into a loose ball. Fold the sides over to the center, turning and pinching to make a tight round ball. Flip the ball, seam-side down, onto the prepared baking sheet.

5 Shape 1 small piece of dough into a ball. Fold the sides over to the center, turning and pinching to make a tight round ball. Set it, seam-side down, on top of the first ball.

6 Holding your forefinger vertically, press the center of the 2 balls down to the bottom of the baking sheet and rotate your finger to enlarge the hole slightly. Repeat to shape the remaining dough.

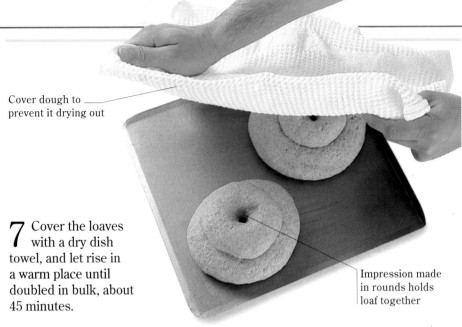

Cover dough to prevent it drying out

7 Cover the loaves with a dry dish towel, and let rise in a warm place until doubled in bulk, about 45 minutes.

Impression made in rounds holds loaf together

8 Heat the oven to 375°F. Bake the loaves in the heated oven until well browned, 40–45 minutes. Turn the loaves over and tap the bottoms with your knuckles. The bread should sound hollow and the sides should feel crisp when pressed. Transfer the loaves to the wire rack and let cool completely.

🍴 TO SERVE
Serve whole wheat bread plain or toasted, with cold beef and horseradish or smoked salmon and cream cheese.

Cottage loaf is cut into thick slices for serving

VARIATION
DOUBLE WHEAT BREAD

Bulghur, wheat kernels that have been steamed, dried, and crushed, adds extra wheat flavor to whole wheat bread. The dough is baked in flower pots.

1 Put 3/4 cup bulghur wheat in a bowl and cover with cold water. Let soak, about 30 minutes. Drain, pressing to extract any excess water.
2 Melt the butter and dissolve the yeast as directed in the main recipe. Put the bulghur wheat in a large bowl. Add the melted butter, remaining honey and water, dissolved yeast, and salt. Stir in the all-purpose and stone-ground whole wheat flours as directed. Knead the dough, and let rise.
3 Heat the oven to 300°F. Soak 2 clean 3-cup clay flower pots in water, about 5 minutes. Put them in the heated oven to dry. Repeat this process twice.
4 Knock the air out of the dough and let rest. Cut it in half, and shape each piece into a ball. Drop the dough into the prepared flower pots, cover, and let rise in a warm place until the pots are just full, about 45 minutes. Heat the oven to 375°F. Bake as directed. Remove the loaves from the pots. The bread should sound hollow when the bottoms are tapped and the sides should feel crisp when pressed. Let cool.

ANNE SAYS
"*Ask at your local garden center for untreated clay flower pots, as some can be toxic. Alternatively, bake the bread in two 1-lb coffee cans. Line each can with buttered parchment paper, extending 2 inches above the rim to form a collar.*"

SOURDOUGH BREAD

 🍽️ MAKES 2 MEDIUM LOAVES 🥣 WORK TIME 45–50 MINUTES* 🍲 BAKING TIME 40–45 MINUTES

EQUIPMENT

bowls, including
two 8-inch bowls

large glass jar,
with lid

roasting pan

2 pieces of
smooth
cotton cloth†

dish towels

wire rack

chef's knife   pastry brush

ladle   utility knife‡

wooden spoon

2 baking sheets

†linen can also be used
‡small knife can also be used

ANNE SAYS
"*Bakers use* bannetons,
*round, linen-lined baskets, to
hold the shape of soft, wet
doughs like sourdough, which
tend to spread as they rise.
These baskets are difficult to
find, so I suggest using round
bowls lined with pieces of
smooth cotton cloth.*"

*The tangy flavor of
bread leavened with
a sourdough starter is
unmistakable. Authentic starter
is made with a flour and water paste which is left
to ferment in the hope of capturing wild airborne
yeast. This method can be unreliable, so I add
some yeast to the starter to encourage
fermentation, and to the dough so it rises evenly.*

GETTING AHEAD

Sourdough starter must be made 3–5 days ahead, and the
sponge 5–8 hours ahead or overnight.

*plus 4–6 days fermenting time for starter and sponge and
2–2 1/2 hours rising time*

SHOPPING LIST

1 1/2 tsp	active dry yeast, or 1/3 oz compressed yeast
1/4 cup	lukewarm water
3 cups	unbleached all-purpose flour, more for bowls
1 tbsp	salt
	vegetable oil for bowl
	yellow cornmeal for baking sheet
	ice cubes
	For the sourdough starter
1 tbsp	active dry yeast, or 2/3 oz compressed yeast
2 cups	lukewarm water
2 cups	unbleached all-purpose flour
	For the sponge
1 cup	lukewarm water
2 cups	unbleached all-purpose flour, more for sprinkling sponge

INGREDIENTS

unbleached all-purpose flour

vegetable oil

active dry yeast

yellow cornmeal

ANNE SAYS
"*Sourdough bread is best
the day of baking, but can
be tightly wrapped and
kept for 2–3 days, or it
can be frozen.*"

ORDER OF WORK

1 MAKE THE
SOURDOUGH
STARTER AND THE
SPONGE

2 MAKE, KNEAD,
AND LET THE
DOUGH RISE

3 SHAPE AND BAKE
THE LOAVES

1 MAKE THE SOURDOUGH STARTER AND THE SPONGE

1 Make the sourdough starter (see box, below). Make the sponge: pour the water into a large bowl and spoon in 1 cup sourdough starter. Stir in the flour and mix vigorously with your hand, 30–60 seconds.

ANNE SAYS
"Remember to replenish the starter after each use."

Remaining starter is kept in jar for future use

Fermented sourdough starter is thick and foamy

2 Sprinkle the sponge with 3 tbsp flour, cover the bowl with a damp dish towel, and let ferment in a warm place, 5–8 hours or overnight.

ANNE SAYS
"If you prefer a more sour flavor, let the sponge ferment overnight."

HOW TO MAKE SOURDOUGH STARTER

This starter can be used within 3–5 days of making. If you don't make sourdough bread frequently, every 2 or 3 weeks stir down the starter to knock out the air, discard half, and replenish it. Let the starter ferment for 1 day at room temperature, then use or refrigerate as directed below. With proper care, the starter will last indefinitely. Discard it if mold appears, or if it gives off a bad, rather than sour, yeasty odor.

Large jar is needed for starter as it ferments

Wooden spoon knocks air out of starter

1 In a large glass jar, sprinkle or crumble the yeast over the water. Let stand until dissolved, stirring once, about 5 minutes.

2 Stir in the flour, cover, and let the starter ferment in a warm place, 24 hours. The starter should become frothy and have a distinct sour odor.

! TAKE CARE !
While the starter ferments, it is important to maintain an even temperature. Keep the jar of starter away from drafts and high heat.

3 Stir down the starter to knock out the air, cover, and let ferment, stirring it each day, 2–4 days longer. Use or refrigerate the starter.

ANNE SAYS
"To keep the starter active and healthy, replenish it after each use. If a recipe calls for 1 cup starter, use it as directed, then stir 1 cup each flour and water back into the jar of starter."

2 MAKE, KNEAD, AND LET THE DOUGH RISE

1 In a small bowl, sprinkle the yeast over the water. Let stand until dissolved, about 5 minutes. Add to the sponge and mix with your hand.

2 Stir in half of the flour, and the salt, and mix well with your hand. Add the remaining flour, 1/2 cup at a time, mixing well after each addition. Keep adding flour until the dough pulls away from the side of the bowl in a ball. It should be soft and slightly sticky.

3 Turn the dough onto a floured work surface. Sprinkle the dough and your hands with flour, and begin to knead by holding the dough with one hand and pushing it away from you with the other. Continue to knead by peeling the dough from the surface. Give the dough a quarter turn, and knead until it is very smooth, elastic, and forms a ball, 8–10 minutes. If the dough sticks while kneading, flour the work surface.

Kneading develops gluten, helping dough to rise

ANNE SAYS
"You can make and knead the dough in a heavy-duty electric mixer fitted with a dough hook."

4 Wash the large bowl and brush it with oil. Put the kneaded dough in the bowl and flip it so it is lightly oiled. Cover the bowl with a damp dish towel and let the dough rise in a warm place until doubled in bulk, 1–1 1/2 hours.

3 SHAPE AND BAKE THE LOAVES

2 Cut the dough in half. Shape each piece of dough into a loose ball. Fold the sides over to the center, turning and pinching to make a tight round ball. Put the balls, seam-side up, into the prepared bowls. Cover with dry dish towels, and let the loaves rise in a warm place until the bowls are just full, about 1 hour.

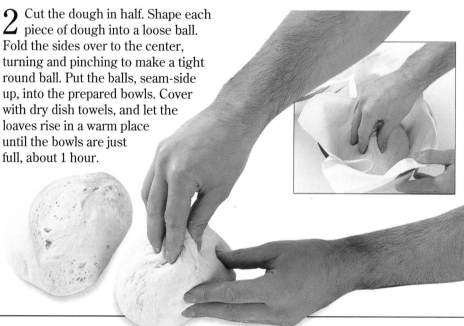

1 Line two 8-inch bowls with the pieces of cloth, and sprinkle generously with flour. Turn the dough onto the lightly floured work surface and knead just to knock out the air, 15–20 seconds. Cover the dough, and let rest, about 5 minutes.

3 Heat the oven to 400°F. Set the roasting pan to heat on the floor of the oven or on the lowest oven rack. Sprinkle the baking sheets with cornmeal. Turn the loaves, seam-side down, out of the bowls, onto the prepared baking sheets. With the utility knife, make 3 parallel slashes, 1/2-inch deep, in the top of each loaf, then make 3 more slashes to form a criss-cross pattern.

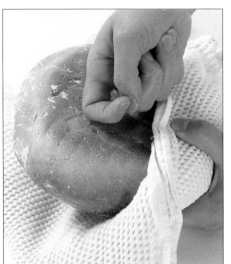

4 Put the loaves in the heated oven. At once drop 10–15 ice cubes into the hot roasting pan, then bake the loaves, 20 minutes. Lower the heat to 375°F and continue baking until well browned, 20–25 minutes longer. Turn the loaves over and tap the bottoms with your knuckles. The bread should sound hollow and the sides should feel crisp when pressed. Transfer the loaves to the wire rack and let cool.

ANNE SAYS
"As the ice cubes hit the hot roasting pan, steam is formed, giving the loaves a crisp crust."

🍽 **TO SERVE**
Serve sourdough bread as an accompaniment to a hearty stew such as seafood cioppino.

Slashes in **dough** make an attractive finish for these loaves

Crisp-crusted **sourdough** has a large, open crumb

V A R I A T I O N

SOURDOUGH ROLLS

Sourdough bread is equally delicious when shaped into individual rolls. Dusted with flour and slashed on top, they are ideal for picnic lunches.

1 Make the starter and the sponge; make, knead, and let the dough rise as directed in the main recipe. Sprinkle 2 baking sheets with cornmeal.

2 Knock the air out of the dough, and let rest as directed. Cut the dough in half. With your hands, roll 1 piece of dough into a cylinder about 2 inches in diameter. With a chef's knife, cut the cylinder into 6 pieces. Repeat to shape and divide the remaining dough.

3 Lightly flour the work surface. Cup a piece of dough under the palm of your hand and roll the dough in a circular motion so it forms a smooth ball. Repeat to shape the remaining dough. Set the rolls on the prepared baking sheets. Cover the rolls with dry dish towels, and let rise in a warm place until doubled in bulk, about 30 minutes.

4 Heat the oven to 400°F, and heat the roasting pan as directed. Lightly sprinkle each roll with flour then, with a utility knife, make an "x" in the center of each roll. Bake as directed, until the rolls are golden and sound hollow when tapped, 25–30 minutes. Makes 12 rolls.

MULTI-GRAIN BREAKFAST BREAD

¶◎¶ MAKES 2 MEDIUM LOAVES   ⌣ WORK TIME 45–50 MINUTES*   ☵ BAKING TIME 40–45 MINUTES

EQUIPMENT

bowls

pastry brush

chef's knife

dish towels

medium saucepan   wire rack

chopping board

2 baking sheets

wooden spoon

This hearty bread combines rolled oats, wheat bran, cornmeal, whole wheat and all-purpose flours, with sunflower seeds for added crunch. Buttermilk softens the texture of the bread, which is shaped to resemble a tobacco pouch.

GETTING AHEAD

This bread is best the day of baking, but can be tightly wrapped and kept for 2–3 days, or it can be frozen.
*plus 2 ½–3 hours rising time

INGREDIENTS

shelled sunflower seeds   unbleached all-purpose flour

yellow cornmeal   wheat bran

active dry yeast   light brown sugar

buttermilk   rolled oats

butter   egg white

whole wheat flour

ANNE SAYS
"Finely crushed bran cereal flakes can be used in place of wheat bran."

ORDER OF WORK

1 PREPARE THE SEEDS; MAKE THE DOUGH AND LET IT RISE

2 SHAPE AND BAKE THE LOAVES

SHOPPING LIST

½ cup	shelled sunflower seeds
1¾ cups	buttermilk
2½ tsp	active dry yeast, or ½ oz compressed yeast
¼ cup	lukewarm water
½ cup	quick-cooking rolled oats
½ cup	wheat bran
½ cup	yellow cornmeal, more for baking sheet
3 tbsp	light brown sugar
1 tbsp	salt
2 cups	whole wheat flour
2 cups	unbleached all-purpose flour, more if needed
	butter for bowl
1	egg white for glaze

1 PREPARE THE SEEDS; MAKE THE DOUGH AND LET IT RISE

1 Heat the oven to 350°F. Spread the sunflower seeds on a baking sheet and toast in the heated oven until lightly browned, stirring occasionally so they color evenly, 5–7 minutes. Let the seeds cool, then coarsely chop.

2 Pour the buttermilk into the saucepan. Heat just to lukewarm. Dissolve the yeast in the water (see box, right).

! TAKE CARE !
High heat will curdle buttermilk.

Buttermilk is used to soften texture of dough

3 Put the sunflower seeds, rolled oats, wheat bran, cornmeal, brown sugar, and salt into a large bowl. Add the dissolved yeast and buttermilk and mix with your hand. Stir in the whole wheat flour with half of the all-purpose flour and mix well with your hand.

5 Keep adding all-purpose flour until the dough pulls away from the side of the bowl in a ball. It should be soft and slightly sticky.

4 Add the remaining all-purpose flour, 1/2 cup at a time, mixing well after each addition.

HOW TO DISSOLVE YEAST

Yeast is a living organism and grows fastest in a warm, moist environment. In bread making, it acts by fermenting the natural sugars in flour into tiny bubbles of carbon dioxide which cause the dough to rise. During baking, the bubbles expand to give bread its characteristic texture and flavor. Yeast is available dried and fresh or compressed. It is activated by being dissolved in a warm liquid, usually water.

1 In a small bowl, sprinkle or crumble yeast over lukewarm liquid.

ANNE SAYS
"*At low temperatures, the yeast works more slowly, and above 130°F most yeast will die. The liquid should be just warm to the touch, 110°–115°F.*"

2 Set aside for 2 minutes. Stir gently with a teaspoon, then leave until the yeast is completely dissolved, 2–3 minutes.

6 Turn the dough onto a floured work surface. Sprinkle the dough and your hands with all-purpose flour, and begin to knead by holding the dough with one hand and pushing it away from you with the other. Continue to knead by peeling the dough from the surface. Give the dough a quarter turn, and knead until it is very smooth, elastic, and forms a ball, 8–10 minutes. If the dough sticks while kneading, flour the work surface.

Push dough firmly against work surface

7 Wash the large bowl and brush it with melted butter. Put the kneaded dough in the bowl, and flip it so the surface is lightly buttered. Cover the bowl with a damp dish towel and let the dough rise in a warm place until doubled in bulk, 1 1/2–2 hours.

2 SHAPE AND BAKE THE LOAVES

1 Sprinkle the baking sheets with cornmeal. Turn the dough onto a lightly floured work surface and knead with your hand just to knock out the air, 15–20 seconds. Cover the dough, and let rest, about 5 minutes.

2 With the chef's knife, cut the dough in half. Flour your hands and pat 1 piece of dough into a 15-x4-inch rectangle, leaving the corners rounded.

4 Cover with dry dish towels, and let the loaves rise in a warm place until doubled in bulk, about 1 hour.

3 Fold the rectangle crosswise in half, gently pressing the halves together. Transfer the loaf to 1 of the prepared baking sheets; repeat to shape the remaining dough.

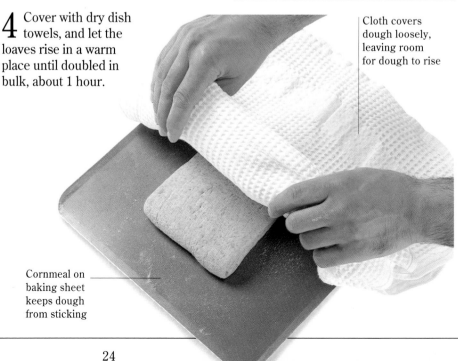

Cloth covers dough loosely, leaving room for dough to rise

Cornmeal on baking sheet keeps dough from sticking

5 Heat the oven to 375°F. Make the glaze: beat the egg white just until frothy. Brush the loaves with the glaze.

Bottom of bread is nicely browned

6 Bake the loaves in the heated oven until well browned, 40–45 minutes. Turn the loaves over and tap the bottoms with your knuckles. The bread should sound hollow and the sides should feel crisp when pressed. Transfer the loaves to the wire rack and let cool completely.

🍴 **TO SERVE**

Serve this hearty bread plain or toasted. It is delicious for breakfast with eggs and bacon.

Egg-white glaze gives bread a shiny finish

Assorted seeds and grains make this a tasty loaf

V A R I A T I O N

ORANGE JUICE BREAKFAST BREAD

Here, orange juice replaces the buttermilk, and the dough is snipped for a decorative "hedgehog" finish. Use freshly squeezed orange juice if you can.

1 Omit the sunflower seeds and buttermilk. Allow 1¾ cups orange juice to come to room temperature. Make the dough, using the orange juice in place of the buttermilk, but do not heat it. Knead the dough, and let rise as directed.

2 Sprinkle a baking sheet with cornmeal. Knock the air out of the dough and let rest as directed. Cut the dough in half. Flour your hands and pat 1 piece of dough into an oval about 10 inches long. Gently roll the dough back and forth on the work surface, exerting more pressure on the ends to taper them. Transfer the loaf to the prepared baking sheet. Repeat to shape the remaining dough. Cover the loaves, and let rise as directed.

3 Heat the oven to 375°F. Glaze the loaves as directed, then snip them deeply all over with kitchen scissors, lifting as you cut to make points of dough. Bake and let cool as directed.

FRENCH BAGUETTE

 MAKES 3   WORK TIME 40–45 MINUTES*   BAKING TIME 25–30 MINUTES

EQUIPMENT

dish towels   3-loaf baguette frame

chef's knife   utility knife†

pastry scraper   pastry brush

roasting pan

wire rack

bowls

†small knife can also be used

ANNE SAYS
"Baguette frames hold the shape of the dough as it rises and bakes, though you may use a cotton cloth and baking sheet instead. Put the cloth on the baking sheet, and flour it generously. Lay the shaped dough on the cloth, pleating the cloth between the pieces of dough, and let rise. To bake, roll the loaves from the cloth onto the baking sheet."

Made simply of flour, water, yeast, and salt, this long crusty loaf is the most renowned of French breads. Leaving the dough to rise three times gives the bread a characteristic open crumb and yeasty flavor – it is certainly worth the time it takes.

GETTING AHEAD
Though this dough takes a long time to rise, some time can be saved by making and kneading the dough in a heavy-duty electric mixer fitted with a dough hook. Baguettes are best within a few hours of baking.
plus 4–5 hours rising time

SHOPPING LIST

2½ tsp	active dry yeast, or ½ oz compressed yeast
1¾ cups	lukewarm water
4 cups	unbleached all-purpose flour, more if needed
2 tsp	salt
	butter for bowl
	ice cubes

INGREDIENTS

unbleached all-purpose flour

active dry yeast

butter

ORDER OF WORK

1 MAKE, KNEAD, AND LET THE DOUGH RISE

2 SHAPE AND BAKE THE BAGUETTES

1 MAKE, KNEAD, AND LET THE DOUGH RISE

Work in any remaining flour while kneading

1 In a small bowl, sprinkle or crumble the yeast over 1/4 cup of the water. Let stand until dissolved, stirring once, about 5 minutes.

2 Put the flour onto the work surface with the salt. Make a large well in the center and add the dissolved yeast and the remaining water. With your fingertips, work the ingredients in the well until thoroughly mixed.

3 Gradually draw in the flour with the pastry scraper and work it into the liquid ingredients with your hand to form a smooth dough. It should be soft and slightly sticky.

Dough becomes less sticky and more elastic during kneading

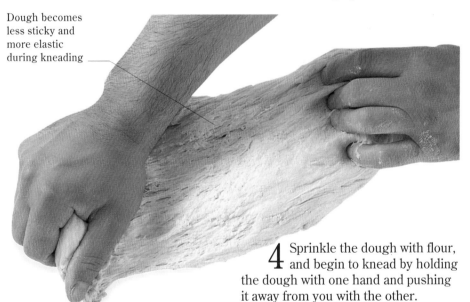

4 Sprinkle the dough with flour, and begin to knead by holding the dough with one hand and pushing it away from you with the other.

5 Continue to knead by peeling the dough from the work surface. Give the dough a quarter turn, and knead until it is very smooth, elastic, and forms a ball, 5–7 minutes. If the dough sticks while kneading, flour the work surface sparingly.

6 Brush a large bowl with melted butter. Put the kneaded dough in the bowl, and flip it so the surface is lightly buttered. Cover the bowl with a damp dish towel and let the dough rise in a warm place until tripled in bulk, 2–2 1/2 hours. Turn the dough onto a lightly floured work surface and knead with your hand just to knock out the air, 15–20 seconds.

7 Return the dough to the bowl, cover, and let rise in a warm place until doubled in bulk, 1–1 1/2 hours.

2 SHAPE AND BAKE THE BAGUETTES

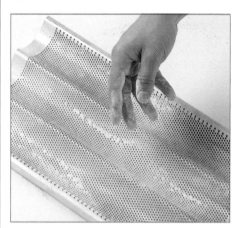

1 Sprinkle the baguette frame with flour. Turn the dough onto a lightly floured work surface and knead with your hand just to knock out the air, 15–20 seconds. Cover the dough, and let rest, about 5 minutes.

2 With the chef's knife, cut straight down through the dough, dividing it into 3 equal pieces.

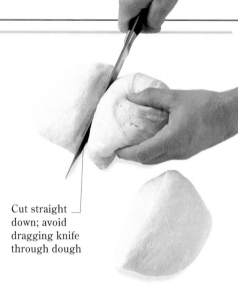

Cut straight down; avoid dragging knife through dough

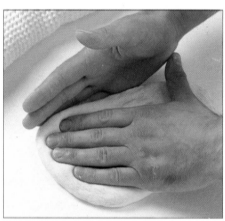

3 Cover 2 pieces of dough while shaping the other. Flour your hands and pat 1 piece of dough into a 7-x 4-inch rectangle.

ANNE SAYS
"Pressing the dough into a rectangle breaks any remaining air pockets, improving its texture."

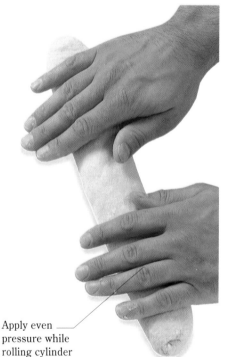

Apply even pressure while rolling cylinder

4 Starting with a long side, roll the rectangle into a cylinder, pinching and sealing it with your fingers as you go. With the palms of your hands, roll the cylinder, stretching it until it is a stick shape about 16 inches long.

ANNE SAYS
"Pinch the cylinder firmly for a well-textured loaf; when rolling, move from the center to the ends to keep the loaf even in shape. Flour hands and work surface as necessary – too much flour and dough will slide, too little and it will stick."

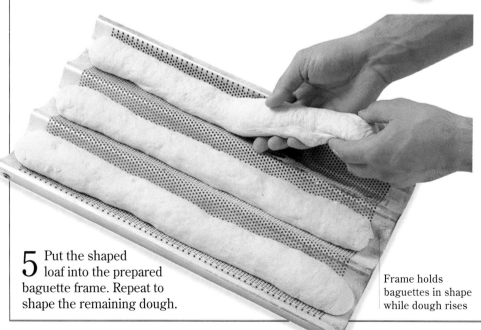

5 Put the shaped loaf into the prepared baguette frame. Repeat to shape the remaining dough.

Frame holds baguettes in shape while dough rises

6 Cover the frame with a dry dish towel, and let the dough rise in a warm place until doubled in bulk, about 1 hour.

7 Heat the oven to 425°F. Set the roasting pan to heat on the floor of the oven or on the lowest oven rack. With the utility knife, make 3 long, slightly diagonal slashes, 1/4-inch deep, in each loaf.

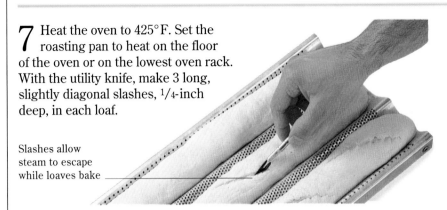

Slashes allow steam to escape while loaves bake

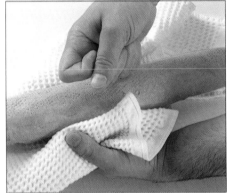

8 Put the frame holding the loaves into the heated oven. At once drop 10–15 ice cubes into the hot roasting pan. Bake the loaves until well browned, 25–30 minutes. Turn them over and tap the bottoms with your knuckles. The bread should sound hollow and the sides should feel crisp when pressed. Let cool completely.

ANNE SAYS
"*As the ice cubes hit the hot roasting pan, steam is formed, giving the loaves a crisp crust.*"

TO SERVE
Baguette is traditionally served plain, but can be split, spread with butter, and layered with ham, pâté, or cheese.

Large, open crumb is characteristic of baguette

Crust is crisp golden-brown

V A R I A T I O N

WHEAT EAR BAGUETTE

These baguettes are shaped to resemble ears of wheat. In France, this bread is called épi.

1 Make, knead, and let the dough rise, first until tripled in bulk, then until doubled, as directed in the main recipe.
2 Press a dry dish towel into the curves of a baguette frame, pleating it between each depression. Sprinkle it generously with flour. Knock the air out of the dough as directed. Shape the loaves, rolling each to a length of 14 inches. Put the loaves in the baguette frame. Let rise as directed.
3 Sprinkle 2 baking sheets with flour. Lift the loaves on the cloth, keeping the pleats intact, onto 1 of the prepared baking sheets. Lift 1 pleat of cloth so 2 loaves roll onto the baking sheet, then arrange them 6 inches apart. Roll the third loaf onto the other baking sheet.
4 Heat the oven and a roasting pan as directed. With kitchen scissors, make a V-shaped cut about halfway through 1 of the loaves, 2–3 inches from the end. Pull the point of the cut section to the left. Make a second cut 2–3 inches from the first, pulling the point to the right. Continue to shape the remaining dough. Bake and let cool as directed.

SEEDED RYE BREAD

🍽️ MAKES 1 MEDIUM LOAF   🥣 WORK TIME 35–40 MINUTES*   ♨️ BAKING TIME 50–55 MINUTES

EQUIPMENT

baking sheet

bowls

wire rack

dish towels

────────
utility knife†

†small knife can also be used

ANNE SAYS
"You can make and knead the dough in a heavy-duty electric mixer fitted with a dough hook, or in a food processor."

Rye flour is darker than wheat flour, producing a crusty loaf that is full of flavor, accented here by caraway seeds. Because rye flour is low in gluten, I've mixed it with all-purpose flour, which is slightly higher in gluten, to lighten the texture of the loaf.

GETTING AHEAD
Rye bread is best the day of baking, but can be tightly wrapped and kept 1–2 days, or it can be frozen.

*plus 2 1/4–2 3/4 hours rising time

INGREDIENTS

caraway seeds   rye flour

unbleached all-purpose flour   egg white

vegetable oil   beer

active dry yeast   yellow cornmeal

molasses

ANNE SAYS
"A Pilsner beer works well for this rye dough."

SHOPPING LIST

2 1/2 tsp	active dry yeast, or 1/2 oz compressed yeast
1/4 cup	lukewarm water
1 tbsp	molasses
1 tbsp	vegetable oil, more for bowl
1 tbsp	caraway seeds
2 tsp	salt
1 cup	beer
2 cups	rye flour
1 1/2 cups	unbleached all-purpose flour, more if needed
	yellow cornmeal for baking sheet
1	egg white for glaze

ORDER OF WORK

1 MAKE, KNEAD, AND LET THE DOUGH RISE

2 SHAPE THE LOAF

3 GLAZE AND BAKE THE LOAF

1 MAKE, KNEAD, AND LET THE DOUGH RISE

1 In a small bowl, sprinkle or crumble the yeast over the water. Let stand until dissolved, stirring once, about 5 minutes.

2 Put the dissolved yeast, molasses, oil, two-thirds of the caraway seeds, and the salt into a large bowl. Pour in the beer. Stir in the rye flour and mix well with your hand.

Beer adds characteristic yeasty flavor

Warmth from your hands helps activate yeast

3 Add the all-purpose flour, 1/2 cup at a time, mixing well after each addition.

4 Keep adding all-purpose flour until the dough pulls away from the side of the bowl in a ball. It should be soft and slightly sticky.

5 Turn the dough onto a floured surface. Sprinkle the dough with flour, and begin to knead by holding the dough with one hand and pushing it away from you with the other.

! TAKE CARE !
Use all-purpose flour for the work surface and your hands.

6 Continue to knead by peeling the dough from the surface. Give the dough a quarter turn, and knead until it is very smooth, elastic, and forms a ball, 8–10 minutes.

ANNE SAYS
"Kneading is more effective when you develop a regular, rhythmic action."

7 Wash the large bowl and brush it with oil. Put the kneaded dough in the bowl, and flip it so the surface is lightly oiled. Cover the bowl with a damp dish towel and let the dough rise in a warm place until doubled in bulk, 1 1/2–2 hours.

2 SHAPE THE LOAF

1 Sprinkle the baking sheet with cornmeal. Turn the dough onto a lightly floured work surface and knead with your hand just to knock out the air, 15–20 seconds. Cover the dough, and let rest, about 5 minutes.

2 Flour your hands and pat the dough into an oval about 10 inches long.

Dough is quickly shaped into rough oval

3 Gently roll the dough back and forth on the work surface, exerting more pressure on the ends to taper them. Transfer the loaf to the prepared baking sheet.

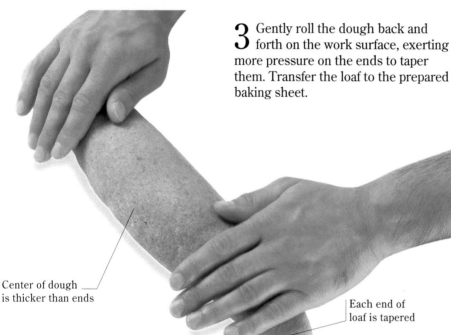

Center of dough is thicker than ends

Each end of loaf is tapered

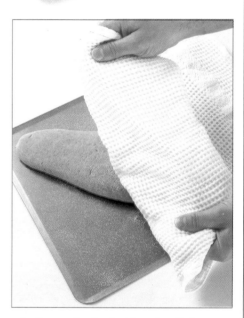

4 Cover the loaf with a dry dish towel, and let rise in a warm place until doubled in bulk, about 45 minutes.

3 GLAZE AND BAKE THE LOAF

2 Sprinkle the loaf with the remaining caraway seeds, and press them into the dough.

Caraway seeds stick easily to egg white

1 Heat the oven to 375°F. Make the glaze: beat the egg white just until frothy. Brush the loaf with the glaze.

3 With the utility knife, make 3 diagonal slashes, about 1/4-inch deep, in the top of the loaf.

Tap center of bread to check if done

Hold hot loaf with dish towel

4 Bake the loaf in the heated oven until well browned, 50–55 minutes. Turn the loaf over and tap the bottom with your knuckles. The bread should sound hollow and the sides should feel crisp when pressed. Transfer the bread to the wire rack and let cool completely.

🍽 TO SERVE

Serve rye bread sliced, as the classic accompaniment to corned beef or pastrami and cole slaw.

Bread is cut into thick slices for serving

Caraway seeds are classic garnish for rye bread

HORSESHOE RYE BREAD

The caraway seeds are omitted in this variation of rye bread. The dough is shaped into a horseshoe for a crusty loaf.

1 Omit the caraway seeds. Make, knead, and let the dough rise as directed.

2 Sprinkle a baking sheet with cornmeal. Knock the air out of the dough, and let rest as directed. Flour your hands and pat the dough into a 10-x8-inch rectangle. Starting with a long side, roll the rectangle into a cylinder, pinching and sealing it with your fingers as you go. With the palms of your hands, roll the cylinder until it is about 18 inches long. Transfer the cylinder, seam-side down, to the prepared baking sheet, then curve the ends around to form a horseshoe.

3 Cover the loaf, and let rise as directed. Heat the oven to 375°F. Make the glaze and brush the loaf with egg white as directed. With a utility knife, make a slash, 1/4-inch deep, along the top, following the curve of the loaf. Bake the loaf, and let cool as directed.

DINNER ROLLS

EQUIPMENT

wooden spoon

chef's knife

saucepan   pastry brush

bowls

2 baking sheets

dish towels

Dinner rolls, made with an egg-enriched dough, are easy to shape. Here you see an assortment – choose your favorite, or make some of each.

GETTING AHEAD

Dinner Rolls are best eaten the day of baking, but the dough can be made, shaped, and frozen ahead of time. Let the rolls come to room temperature, 2½–3 hours, then glaze and bake them just before serving. The freshly baked rolls also freeze well.

*plus 1½–2 hours rising time

SHOPPING LIST

1 cup	milk
¼ cup	unsalted butter, more for bowl and baking sheets
2 tbsp	sugar
2½ tsp	active dry yeast, or ½ oz compressed yeast
2	eggs
2 tsp	salt
4½ cups	unbleached all-purpose flour, more if needed
	For the glaze
1	egg yolk
1 tbsp	water
	poppy seeds for sprinkling (optional)

INGREDIENTS

egg yolk   eggs

unsalted butter   active dry yeast

milk

unbleached all-purpose flour

sugar

poppy seeds

ORDER OF WORK

1. MAKE, KNEAD, AND LET THE DOUGH RISE

2. SHAPE AND BAKE THE ROLLS

1 MAKE, KNEAD, AND LET THE DOUGH RISE

1 Put the milk into the saucepan and bring just to a boil. Pour 1/4 cup of the milk into a small bowl and let cool to lukewarm. Meanwhile, cut the butter into pieces.

2 Add the butter and sugar to the remaining milk in the pan, stirring occasionally, until the butter is melted. Let cool to lukewarm.

3 Sprinkle the yeast over the 1/4 cup milk and let stand, stirring once, until dissolved, about 5 minutes.

! TAKE CARE !
Milk that is too hot may kill the yeast.

4 In a large bowl, beat the eggs just until mixed. Add the cooled sweetened milk, salt, and dissolved yeast.

Liquid ingredients are combined first

Mix dough vigorously with hand

5 Stir in half of the flour and mix well with your hand. Add the remaining flour, 1/2 cup at a time, mixing well after each addition. Keep adding flour until the dough pulls away from the side of the bowl in a ball. It should be soft and slightly sticky.

Kneading develops gluten, helping dough to rise

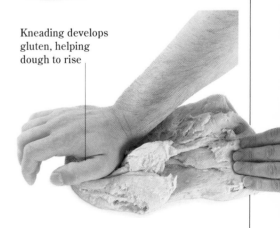

6 Turn the dough onto a floured work surface. Sprinkle the dough and your hands with flour, and begin to knead by holding the dough with one hand and pushing it away from you with the other.

Dough is smooth from kneading

Light coating of butter will keep dough moist

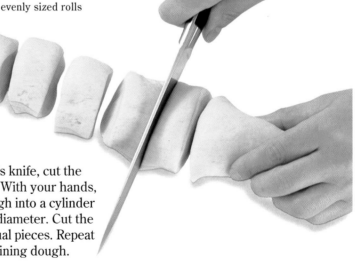

7 Continue to knead by peeling the dough from the surface. Give the dough a quarter turn, and knead until it is very smooth, elastic, and forms a ball, 5–7 minutes. If the dough sticks while kneading, flour the work surface.

8 Wash the large bowl and brush it with melted butter. Put the kneaded dough in the bowl, and flip it so the surface is lightly buttered. Cover the bowl with a damp dish towel and let the dough rise in a warm place until doubled in bulk, 1–1 1/2 hours.

2 SHAPE AND BAKE THE ROLLS

Equal pieces of dough will make evenly sized rolls

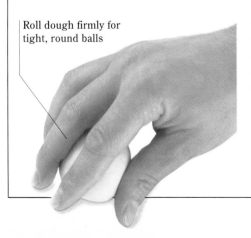

Roll dough firmly for tight, round balls

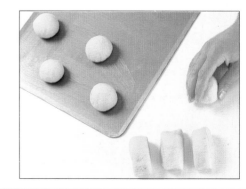

1 Brush the baking sheets with melted butter. Turn the dough onto a lightly floured work surface and knead with your hand just to knock out the air, 15–20 seconds. Cover the dough, and let rest, about 5 minutes.

2 With the chef's knife, cut the dough in half. With your hands, roll 1 piece of dough into a cylinder about 2 inches in diameter. Cut the cylinder into 8 equal pieces. Repeat to divide the remaining dough.

3 To shape round rolls, cup a piece of dough under the palm of your hand, and roll the dough in a circular motion so it forms a smooth ball. For other shapes, see box, page 37.

4 Arrange 8 rolls on each baking sheet. Cover with a dry dish towel, and let rise in a warm place until doubled in bulk, about 30 minutes.

DECORATIVE ROLLS

Rolls are easy to shape. Choose your favorite, or make some of each. When shaping the dough, use only a small amount of flour on your hands and on the work surface: too much flour will change the consistency of the dough, making it dry and stiff.

PARKER HOUSE

1 Make a round roll, then pat it out flat, until ³/₈-inch thick.

2 Brush the round with melted butter, fold, and press.

BOW KNOT

1 Roll a piece of dough into a long rope.

2 Tie a single knot, pulling through the ends of the rope.

BAKER'S KNOT

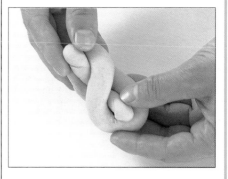

1 Roll a piece of dough into a long rope.

2 Shape into a figure of eight, and tuck the ends through the holes.

TWIST

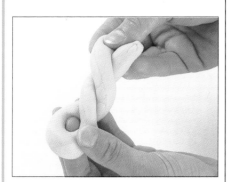

1 Roll a piece of dough into a long rope, fold it in half, and twist.

2 Arrange the twist on a baking sheet and press down the ends.

SNAIL

1 Roll a piece of dough into a long rope.

2 Wind the rope around in a spiral, tucking the end underneath.

CLOVER LEAF

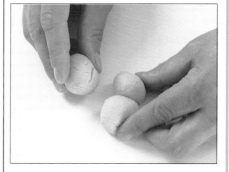

1 Divide a piece of dough into thirds and shape into small balls.

2 Push the balls close together so they are touching.

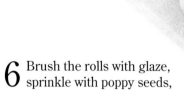

Brush tops
and sides of
dough with
glaze

6 Brush the rolls with glaze, sprinkle with poppy seeds, if you like, then bake them in the heated oven until golden brown, 15–18 minutes.

5 Heat the oven to 425°F. Make the glaze: beat the egg yolk with the water until frothy.

7 Turn over the rolls and tap the bottoms with your knuckles. They should sound hollow when tapped.

Tap center
of roll

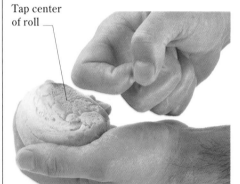

Egg glaze bakes
to a golden brown

🍽 **TO SERVE**
Serve the rolls warm from the oven, piled in a basket. Spread them with butter, if you like.

Poppy seeds make
an attractive
decoration for rolls

CHALLAH

This traditional Jewish bread is baked for holidays and the Sabbath. It is usually, but not always, braided. Challah, meaning offering in Hebrew, dates from the third century BC, when Jews baked the loaves to bring to the temple.

1 Make the dough, using 1 cup lukewarm water instead of milk, ¼ cup vegetable oil instead of butter, and an additional 2 tbsp sugar. Knead, and let the dough rise as directed. Brush a baking sheet with oil. Knock the air out of the dough, and let rest.

2 Cut the dough into 4 equal pieces. Flour the work surface. Roll each piece of dough with the palms of your hands, stretching it to form a 25-inch strand. Make a braided loaf with the strands of dough (see box, below). Transfer the loaf to the prepared baking sheet.

3 Cover with a dry dish towel, and let rise until doubled in bulk, about 45 minutes. Heat the oven to 375°F. Glaze as directed, sprinkle with 1 tsp poppy seeds, and bake until golden and the bread sounds hollow when the bottom is tapped, 35–40 minutes.

HOW TO MAKE A BRAIDED LOAF

Braided loaves are usually made using 3 or 4 strands of dough. More decorative loaves are made with as many as 8 or 12 strands.

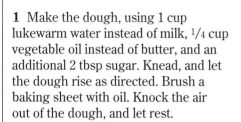

1 Line the strands up next to each other. Starting from your left, lift the first strand to cross over the second.

2 Lift the third strand to cross over the fourth. Now lift the fourth strand to lay between the first and second strands.

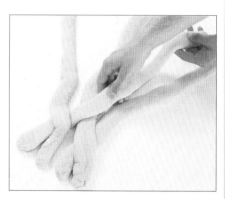

3 Continue braiding: starting again from your left, lift the first strand to cross over the second. Lift the third strand to cross over the fourth. Now lift the fourth strand to lay between the first and second strands.

Braid strands as evenly as possible

4 Finish braiding the strands, pinching the ends together and tucking them under the braided loaf.

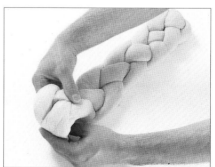

KUGELHOPF WITH WALNUTS, BACON, AND HERBS

🍴 MAKES 1 LARGE LOAF   🥄 WORK TIME 45–50 MINUTES*   🍲 BAKING TIME 45–50 MINUTES

EQUIPMENT

1-quart kugelhopf mold†

chef's knife

pastry brush

wire rack

saucepan

strainer

dish towels

paper towels

frying pan

pastry scraper

chopping board

bowls

slotted spoon

† 1-quart bundt mold can also be used

INGREDIENTS

bacon

walnut halves

fresh thyme

fresh sage

unsalted butter

active dry yeast

eggs

milk

unbleached all-purpose flour

sugar

This yeast bread from Alsace, the most easterly province of France, is traditionally baked in a fluted ring mold. Slice the bread to reveal savory walnuts, bacon, and fresh herbs.

GETTING AHEAD
Kugelhopf is best the day of baking, but can be tightly wrapped and kept 2–3 days, or it can be frozen.

*plus 1 1/2–2 1/4 hours rising time

SHOPPING LIST

1 cup	milk
2/3 cup	unsalted butter, more for kugelhopf mold
1 tbsp	sugar
1 tbsp	active dry yeast, or 2/3 oz compressed yeast
3	eggs
4 cups	unbleached all-purpose flour
1 tsp	salt
3–5	sprigs of fresh sage
3–5	sprigs of fresh thyme
1/2 cup	walnut halves
4 oz	thick-cut bacon slices

ORDER OF WORK

1   MAKE, KNEAD, AND LET THE DOUGH RISE

2   PREPARE OTHER INGREDIENTS

3   FINISH AND BAKE THE KUGELHOPF

1 MAKE, KNEAD, AND LET THE DOUGH RISE

1 Bring the milk just to a boil, pour ¼ cup into a bowl, and let cool to lukewarm. Cut the butter into pieces. Add the butter and sugar to the milk in the pan, stirring until melted. Let cool.

2 Sprinkle the yeast over the ¼ cup milk and let stand until dissolved, stirring once, about 5 minutes.

! TAKE CARE !
Milk that is too hot may kill the yeast.

4 With your fingertips, work the ingredients in the well until thoroughly mixed.

5 Gradually draw in the flour and work it into the other ingredients with your hand to form a smooth dough.

3 Beat the eggs just until mixed. Sift the flour and salt into a large bowl. Make a well in the center and add the dissolved yeast, eggs, and the cooled sweetened milk.

Dough will become more elastic during kneading

6 Beat the dough: cupping your hand like a spoon, lift the dough, then let it fall back into the bowl with a slap. Continue beating the dough until it is very elastic, 5–7 minutes. You may tilt the bowl slightly to make beating easier.

! TAKE CARE !
Do not be tempted to add more flour to this dough when kneading; it should be very sticky.

7 Cover the bowl with a damp dish towel and let the dough rise in a warm place until doubled in bulk, 1–1½ hours. Meanwhile, prepare the other ingredients.

ANNE SAYS
"The flavor of the dough develops as the dough rises."

HOW TO CHOP HERBS

Sage, thyme, parsley, rosemary, and tarragon are herbs that are usually chopped before being added to other ingredients. Do not chop delicate herbs like basil too finely because they bruise easily.

1 Strip the leaves or sprigs from the stems. Pile the leaves or sprigs on a chopping board.

2 With a chef's knife, cut the herbs into small pieces. Holding the tip of the blade against the board and rocking the knife back and forth, chop until the herbs are coarse or fine.

ANNE SAYS
"*Make sure your knife is very sharp, otherwise you will bruise the herbs rather than cut them.***"**

2 PREPARE OTHER INGREDIENTS

1 Brush the kugelhopf mold with melted butter. Freeze the mold until the butter is hard, about 10 minutes, then butter it again.

2 Chop the herbs (see box, left). Set 5 walnut halves aside for decoration. With the chef's knife, coarsely chop the remaining walnuts.

3 Stack the bacon slices on the chopping board and cut them crosswise into strips. Cook the bacon, stirring occasionally, until lightly browned, 3–4 minutes. With the slotted spoon, transfer the bacon to paper towels to drain.

Paper towel absorbs excess bacon fat

3 FINISH AND BAKE THE KUGELHOPF

1 Beat the dough lightly with your hand just to knock out the air, 15–20 seconds. Add the herbs, chopped walnuts, and bacon and beat with your hand until well combined.

2 Arrange the reserved walnut halves in a circle in the bottom of the prepared mold, placing them rounded-side down in the depressions.

3 Using the pastry scraper, drop the dough into the mold, filling it evenly. Cover the mold with a dry dish towel, and let the dough rise in a warm place until just above the top of the mold, 30–40 minutes.

Drop dough gently to keep walnut halves in place

4 Heat the oven to 375°F. Bake the kugelhopf in the heated oven until puffed and very brown, and the bread starts to shrink from the side of the mold, 45–50 minutes. Let cool slightly. Unmold the bread onto the wire rack and let cool completely.

🍴 TO SERVE

Serve the kugelhopf sliced, as an accompaniment to soups or simple salads.

Walnut halves are attractive decoration for buttery kugelhopf

Bacon is savory and tender

V A R I A T I O N

KUGELHOPF WITH RAISINS AND ALMONDS

Dark raisins and chopped almonds are baked in this sweet kugelhopf – an Alsatian classic. A dusting of confectioners' sugar hints at the sweet filling.

1 Omit the herbs, walnuts, and bacon. Bring the milk just to a boil. Let 1/4 cup of the milk cool to lukewarm. Melt the butter as directed, adding 1/3 cup granulated sugar. Dissolve the yeast; make, knead, and let the dough rise as directed in the main recipe.

2 Prepare the kugelhopf mold as directed. Put 1/2 cup raisins in a small bowl and pour over hot water to cover. Let the raisins soak until plump, 10–15 minutes, then drain thoroughly. Set 7 whole blanched almonds aside for decoration. Coarsely chop 1/2 cup whole blanched almonds. Arrange the reserved almonds, alternating with 7 soaked raisins, in the bottom of the prepared mold.

3 Mix the remaining raisins and chopped almonds into the kugelhopf dough in place of the herbs, walnuts, and bacon. Finish, bake, and unmold the kugelhopf as directed. Just before serving, with a small strainer, sift 1 tbsp confectioners' sugar over the kugelhopf.

ONION AND WALNUT CROWN

MAKES 1 LARGE LOAF   **WORK TIME 40–45 MINUTES***   **BAKING TIME 45–50 MINUTES**

EQUIPMENT

bowls

kitchen scissors

pastry brush

chef's knife

pastry scraper

saucepan

wire rack

dish towels

frying pan

baking sheet

chopping board

wooden spoon

ANNE SAYS
"You can make and knead the dough in a heavy-duty electric mixer fitted with a dough hook."

Onions and walnuts, among my favorite produce from the southwest of France, work well together to flavor this simple white loaf. The onions are first sautéed, and the walnuts toasted, before being kneaded into the dough. The loaf is fashioned into a crown and scored for a decorative finish.

GETTING AHEAD
Onion bread is best the day of baking, but can be tightly wrapped and kept for 2–3 days, or it can be frozen.
*plus 1 3/4–2 1/4 hours rising time

SHOPPING LIST

1 3/4 cups	milk, more for glaze
2 1/2 tsp	active dry yeast, or 1/2 oz compressed yeast
2 tbsp	vegetable oil, more for bowl and baking sheet
2 tsp	salt
4 cups	unbleached all-purpose flour, more if needed
1	large onion
	pepper
1/2 cup	walnut pieces

INGREDIENTS

onion

walnut pieces

active dry yeast

milk

vegetable oil

unbleached all-purpose flour

ORDER OF WORK

1 **MAKE, KNEAD, AND LET THE DOUGH RISE**

2 **PREPARE THE ONION AND WALNUTS**

3 **SHAPE AND BAKE THE CROWN**

---

1 MAKE, KNEAD, AND LET THE DOUGH RISE

1 Bring the milk just to a boil. Pour ¼ cup of the milk into a small bowl and let cool to lukewarm.

2 Sprinkle or crumble the yeast over the ¼ cup milk, and let stand until dissolved, stirring once, about 5 minutes.

! TAKE CARE !
Milk that is too hot may kill the yeast.

Beat vigorously with hand for even mixing

3 Put the dissolved yeast, remaining milk, half of the oil, and the salt into a large bowl. Stir in half of the flour and mix well with your hand.

4 Add the remaining flour, ½ cup at a time, mixing well after each addition. Keep adding flour until the dough pulls away from the side of the bowl in a ball. It should be soft and slightly sticky.

ANNE SAYS
"If flour remains, work it in while kneading the dough."

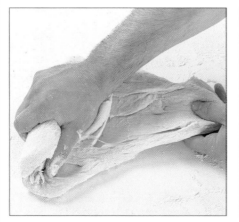

5 Turn the dough onto a floured work surface. Sprinkle the dough and your hands with flour, and begin to knead by holding the dough with one hand and pushing it away from you with the other.

6 Continue to knead by peeling the dough from the surface. Give the dough a quarter turn, and knead until it is very smooth, elastic, and forms a ball, 5–7 minutes. If the dough sticks while kneading, flour the work surface.

Damp dish towel helps prevent dough from drying out

7 Wash the large bowl and brush it with melted butter. Flip the dough in the bowl so it is lightly buttered. Cover with a damp dish towel and let rise in a warm place until doubled in bulk, 1–1½ hours.

2 PREPARE THE ONION AND WALNUTS

Use knuckles to guide knife

1 Heat the oven to 350°F. Peel the onion, and cut it lengthwise in half. Set each half cut-side down and slice horizontally, then vertically toward the root, leaving the slices attached. Cut across into dice. Chop until fine.

2 Heat the remaining oil in the frying pan. Add the chopped onion with salt and pepper and cook, stirring often, until soft and lightly brown, 5–7 minutes. Taste for seasoning and set aside to cool.

3 Spread the walnut pieces on the baking sheet and toast in the heated oven, stirring occasionally, until lightly browned, 8–10 minutes. Let the nuts cool, then coarsely chop them with the chef's knife.

3 SHAPE AND BAKE THE CROWN

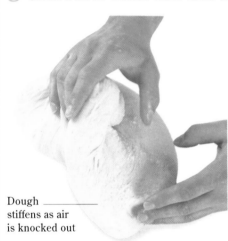

Dough stiffens as air is knocked out

1 Brush the baking sheet with oil. Turn the dough onto a lightly floured work surface and knead with your hand just to knock out the air, 15–20 seconds. Cover the dough, and let rest, about 5 minutes.

2 Knead the onion and walnuts into the dough until evenly blended, 2–3 minutes. Cover the dough, and let rest, about 5 minutes longer.

Use fingers to shape and stretch center of ring

3 Shape the dough into a loose ball. Fold the sides over to the center, turning and pinching to make a tight round ball. Flip the ball, seam-side down, onto the work surface.

4 Make a hole in the center of the ball with two of your fingers. With your fingers, enlarge the hole, turning to make an even ring. Gradually enlarge the ring to a diameter of 10–12 inches.

5 Lift the ring onto the prepared baking sheet. Cover the ring with a dry dish towel, and let rise in a warm place until doubled in bulk, about 45 minutes.

6 Heat the oven to 400°F. Brush the ring with milk. With the kitchen scissors, snip around the top of the ring in a zig-zag design.

Cut about 1/4 inch into dough

7 Bake the loaf in the heated oven until it is well browned, 45–50 minutes. Turn the bread over and tap the bottom with your knuckles. The bread should sound hollow and the sides should feel crisp when pressed. Transfer the bread to the wire rack and let cool completely.

🍴 **TO SERVE**
Serve this bread plain or buttered, or as part of a ploughman's lunch of salad greens, hard cheese, chutney, and pickles.

Toasted walnuts, together with sautéed onions, add rich flavor to this simple white bread

---

V A R I A T I O N

GREEN AND BLACK OLIVE BREAD

Oil-cured green and black olives give this loaf a pungent, earthy flavor.

1 Omit the milk, vegetable oil, onion, pepper, and walnuts. Make the dough, using 1 1/2 cups lukewarm water in place of the milk and 1 tbsp olive oil instead of the vegetable oil. Knead the dough, and let rise as directed.
2 Meanwhile, pit and coarsely chop 1/2 cup oil-cured green olives and 1/2 cup oil-cured black olives. Brush a baking sheet with oil.
3 Knock the air out of the dough and let rest as directed. Knead the chopped olives into the dough as for the onion and walnuts, and let rest as directed. Flour your hands and pat the dough into an oval about 10 inches long. Gently roll the dough back and forth on the work surface. Transfer the dough to the prepared baking sheet. Cover the loaf and let rise as directed.
4 Heat the oven to 400°F. Sprinkle the loaf with flour. With a chef's knife, make a slash down the center of the loaf, cutting all the way through the dough to the baking sheet. Bake the loaf and let cool as directed.

SMALL BRIOCHES

 MAKES 10   WORK TIME 45–50 MINUTES*   BAKING TIME 15–20 MINUTES

EQUIPMENT

wire rack

ten 3-inch brioche molds

chef's knife

pastry brush   dish towels

bowls   strainer

baking sheet

pastry scraper

INGREDIENTS

eggs   unsalted butter

unbleached all-purpose flour

sugar

active dry yeast

Famous for its shape, brioche is a classic French bread, rich with eggs and butter. Traditionally it is formed with a round "head" on top, then baked in a scalloped mold. Here, small molds are used.

GETTING AHEAD

Brioches are best freshly baked, or can be frozen. The dough can be made, kneaded, and left in the refrigerator to rise overnight. Let the dough come to room temperature, knead in the butter, and finish the brioches as directed.

*plus 1 1/2–2 hours rising time

SHOPPING LIST

2 1/2 tsp	active dry yeast, or 1/2 oz compressed yeast
2 tbsp	lukewarm water
5	eggs
3 cups	unbleached all-purpose flour, more if needed
2 tbsp	sugar
1 1/2 tsp	salt
3/4 cup	unsalted butter, softened, more for bowl and brioche molds
	For the glaze
1	egg
1/2 tsp	salt

ORDER OF WORK

1 MAKE, KNEAD, AND LET THE DOUGH RISE

2 KNEAD IN THE BUTTER

3 SHAPE AND BAKE THE BRIOCHES

ANNE SAYS
"You can make, knead, and work the butter into the dough in a heavy-duty electric mixer fitted with a dough hook, or in a food processor."

1 MAKE, KNEAD, AND LET THE DOUGH RISE

1 In a small bowl, sprinkle or crumble the yeast over the water. Let stand until dissolved, stirring once, about 5 minutes.

2 In a small bowl, beat the eggs with a fork just until mixed.

3 Sift the flour onto the work surface with the sugar and salt. Make a large well in the center and add the eggs and dissolved yeast. With your fingertips, work the ingredients in the well until thoroughly mixed.

Large well is needed to hold liquid ingredients

Beaten eggs add characteristic richness to brioche dough

4 Gradually draw in the flour with the pastry scraper and work it into the other ingredients with your hand to form a smooth dough. It should be soft and sticky.

5 Sprinkle the dough with flour and knead, lifting the dough up and throwing it down until it is very elastic and resembles chamois leather, 8–10 minutes. Work in more flour as necessary, so that at the end of kneading the dough is slightly sticky but peels easily from the work surface. It will become less sticky and more elastic while kneading, so add flour sparingly.

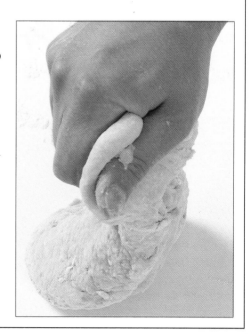

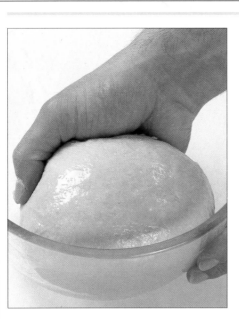

Damp dish towel keeps dough moist while it rises

Dough is lightly coated with melted butter

6 Brush a large bowl with melted butter. Put the kneaded dough into the bowl, and flip it, rolling it against the side of the bowl so the surface is lightly buttered.

7 Cover the bowl with a damp dish towel and let the dough rise in a warm place until doubled in bulk, 1–1 1/2 hours. Alternatively, put the covered bowl of dough in the refrigerator and leave it up to 8 hours or overnight. It will rise slowly during this time.

2 KNEAD IN THE BUTTER

1 Brush the brioche molds with melted butter. Set the molds on the baking sheet.

Pastry brush reaches every part of mold

Double coating of melted butter prevents brioche sticking to mold

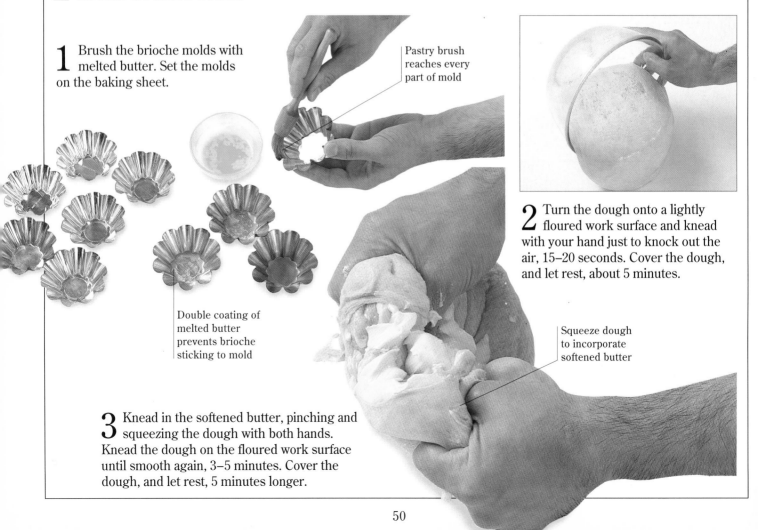

2 Turn the dough onto a lightly floured work surface and knead with your hand just to knock out the air, 15–20 seconds. Cover the dough, and let rest, about 5 minutes.

Squeeze dough to incorporate softened butter

3 Knead in the softened butter, pinching and squeezing the dough with both hands. Knead the dough on the floured work surface until smooth again, 3–5 minutes. Cover the dough, and let rest, 5 minutes longer.

3 SHAPE AND BAKE THE BRIOCHES

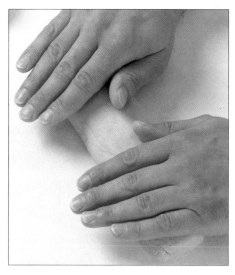

Dough is fairly stiff and will hold its shape

1 Cut the dough in half. Roll 1 piece of dough into a cylinder about 2 inches in diameter. Cut the cylinder into 5 pieces. Repeat to shape and divide the remaining dough.

2 Lightly flour the work surface. Cup each piece of dough under the palm of your hand and roll the dough in a circular motion so it forms a smooth ball.

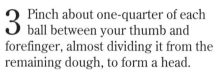

3 Pinch about one-quarter of each ball between your thumb and forefinger, almost dividing it from the remaining dough, to form a head.

4 Holding the head, lower each ball into a mold, twisting and pressing the head onto the base of the brioche.

Cover loosely with dish towel so brioches have room to rise

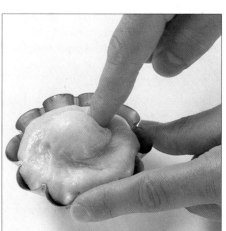

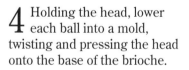

5 With your forefinger, press down 2–3 times around each head to seal it to the base of the brioche.

6 Cover the molds with a dry dish towel, and let the dough rise in a warm place until the molds are full and the dough is puffed, about 30 minutes.

8 Unmold 1 of the brioches, turn it over, and tap the bottom with your knuckles. It should sound hollow. Let the brioches cool slightly, then unmold them. Transfer to the wire rack and let cool completely.

Hold hot brioche with dish towel

Side and bottom of brioche are golden brown

7 Heat the oven to 425°F. Make the egg glaze: lightly beat the egg with the salt. Brush the brioches with glaze. Bake the brioches in the heated oven until puffed and brown, 15–20 minutes.

ANNE SAYS
"*Good-quality butter makes the best brioche. Normandy and the Charentes, where the best French butter comes from, pride themselves on their brioche.*"

🍽 **TO SERVE**
Brioches make a special breakfast or afternoon tea. Serve them plain, or with jam to spread on each bite.

Brioche is shaped with characteristic head on top

Egg glaze bakes to a rich golden brown

RICH BRIOCHE

Here, brioche dough is shaped into large round loaves – its classic guise. More butter is kneaded in to make this variation quite rich. Serve it sliced, toasted, and spread with jam.

1 Make, knead, and let the dough rise as directed in the main recipe.
2 Brush two 7-inch brioche molds with melted butter. Knock the air out of the dough and let it rest as directed. Work 1 cup plus 1 tbsp softened unsalted butter into the dough until smooth.
3 Cut the dough in half. Pinch off one-third of each piece for the heads of the brioches. Shape all 4 pieces of dough into tight round balls. Put the large balls, seam-side down, into the prepared brioche molds, making a depression in the center of each ball. Set the small balls on top, pressing them to the bases as directed. Cover the molds and let the dough rise in a warm place until the molds are full, about 45 minutes.
4 Heat the oven to 400°F. Make the egg glaze and glaze the brioches as directed. Bake the loaves until puffed and brown, 25–30 minutes. Unmold the loaves, turn them over, and tap the bottoms with your knuckles. They should sound hollow when tapped. Let cool as directed. Makes 2 loaves.

CHEESE BRIOCHE

Brie cheese adds ripe flavor to brioche when kneaded into the dough in place of some of the butter. Baked in a loaf pan, this rich bread is excellent sliced to eat plain or toasted.

1 Make, knead, and let the dough rise as directed in the main recipe. Brush a 9-x5-x3-inch loaf pan with melted butter. Cut the rind from 5 oz Brie cheese, cut the cheese into small chunks, and let it come to room temperature. Knock the air out of the dough, and let rest as directed. Work the cheese and 1/4 cup softened unsalted butter into the dough until smooth.
2 Cut the dough in half. Roll each piece into a cylinder and cut each cylinder into 4 pieces. Roll each piece of dough into a ball as directed, but do not form a head. Put the balls of dough into the prepared pan, arranging them on a slight diagonal. Cover the pan as directed, and let the dough rise in a warm place until the pan is three-quarters full, about 45 minutes.
3 Heat the oven to 400°F. Glaze the loaf as directed. Bake the loaf until well browned and the brioche sounds hollow when the bottom is tapped, 30–35 minutes. Transfer to a wire rack and let cool completely. Makes 1 loaf.

POTATO-CHIVE MONKEY BREAD

 MAKES 1 LARGE LOAF   WORK TIME 50–55 MINUTES*   BAKING TIME 40–45 MINUTES

EQUIPMENT

1³/₄-quart ring mold

bowls

wire rack

dish towels

strainer

chopping board

potato masher

chef's knife

pastry brush

vegetable peeler

pastry scraper

small saucepan with lid

shallow dish

ANNE SAYS
"*You can make and knead the dough in a heavy-duty electric mixer fitted with a dough hook, or in a food processor. If you do not have a ring mold, you can use a 10-inch round cake pan, setting a 1-cup ramekin upside down in the center.*"

Bread made with mashed potato, long an American favorite, has a soft crust and moist center. In this recipe, fresh chives are kneaded into the dough, which is shaped into balls, coated in butter, and baked in a ring mold. The result is "monkey" bread, served by simply pulling it apart with your fingers.

GETTING AHEAD

Potato bread is delicious warm from the oven, but can be tightly wrapped and kept 2–3 days, or it can be frozen. The dough can be made, kneaded, and left to rise in the refrigerator overnight. Shape the dough, let it come to room temperature, then bake as directed.

*plus 1 ¹/₂–2 ¹/₄ hours rising time

SHOPPING LIST

¹/₂ lb	potatoes
2 ¹/₂ tsp	active dry yeast or ¹/₂ oz compressed yeast
¹/₄ cup	lukewarm water
¹/₂ cup	unsalted butter, more for bowl and ring mold
1	large bunch of chives
2 tbsp	sugar
2 tsp	salt
3 ¹/₂ cups	unbleached all-purpose flour, more if needed

INGREDIENTS

potatoes

chives

unsalted butter

active dry yeast

unbleached all-purpose flour

sugar

ORDER OF WORK

1 PREPARE THE POTATOES AND MAKE THE DOUGH

2 KNEAD AND LET THE DOUGH RISE

3 SHAPE AND BAKE THE LOAF

1 PREPARE THE POTATOES AND MAKE THE DOUGH

1 Peel the potatoes and cut them into 2–3 pieces. Put them in the saucepan with plenty of cold water, cover, and bring to a boil. Simmer just until they are tender when pierced with the tip of a knife, 15–20 minutes.

2 Drain the potatoes, reserving 1 cup of the cooking liquid. Mash the potatoes with the potato masher. There should be $^3/_4$ cup mashed potato. Let the reserved liquid and the potatoes cool.

3 In a small bowl, sprinkle or crumble the yeast over the water. Let stand until dissolved, stirring once, about 5 minutes.

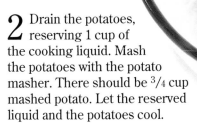

4 Melt half of the butter in the saucepan. Meanwhile, finely chop the chives.

ANNE SAYS
"Wash and dry the chives before chopping only if they are dirty."

5 Put the reserved potato liquid, mashed potato, dissolved yeast, and melted butter into a large bowl. Add the chopped chives, sugar, and salt and mix with your hand.

6 Stir in half of the flour and mix well with your hand. Add the remaining flour, $^1/_2$ cup at a time, mixing well after each addition. Keep adding flour until the dough pulls away from the side of the bowl in a ball. It should be soft and slightly sticky.

2 KNEAD AND LET THE DOUGH RISE

1 Turn the dough onto a floured work surface. Sprinkle the dough and your hands with flour, and begin to knead by holding the dough with one hand and pushing it away from you with the other.

2 Continue to knead by peeling the dough from the surface. Give the dough a quarter turn, and knead until it is very smooth, elastic, and forms a ball, 5–7 minutes. If the dough sticks while kneading, flour the work surface.

3 Wash the large bowl and brush it with melted butter. Put the kneaded dough in the bowl, and flip it so the surface is lightly buttered. Cover the bowl with a damp dish towel and let the dough rise in a warm place until doubled in bulk, 1–1 1/2 hours.

3 SHAPE AND BAKE THE LOAF

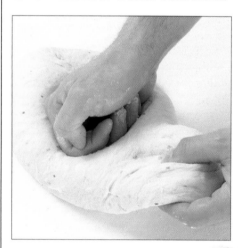

1 Brush the ring mold with melted butter. Melt the remaining 1/4 cup butter and pour it into the shallow dish. Turn the dough onto a lightly floured work surface and knead with your hand just to knock out the air, 15–20 seconds. Cover the dough and let rest, about 5 minutes.

2 Flour your hands and pinch off walnut-sized pieces of dough, making about 30 pieces.

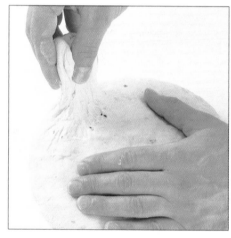

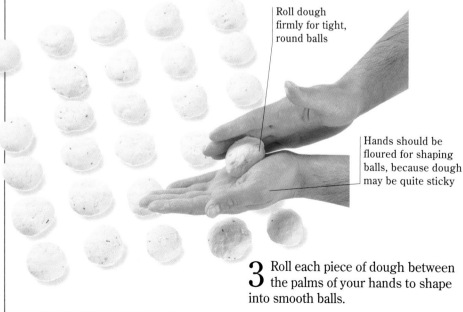

Roll dough firmly for tight, round balls

Hands should be floured for shaping balls, because dough may be quite sticky

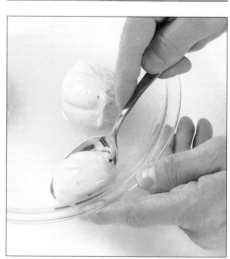

3 Roll each piece of dough between the palms of your hands to shape into smooth balls.

4 Put a few balls of dough into the dish of melted butter and turn them with a spoon until coated.

5 Transfer the balls of dough to the prepared mold. Repeat with the remaining dough. Cover the mold with a dry dish towel, and let the loaf rise in a warm place until the mold is full, about 40 minutes.

Use spoon to drop buttered balls of dough into mold

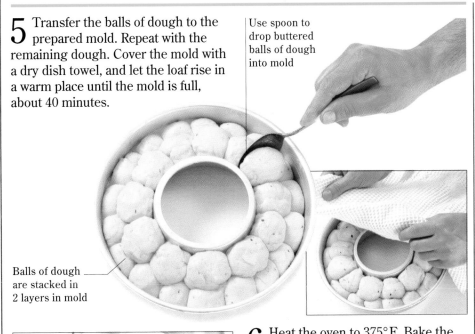

Balls of dough are stacked in 2 layers in mold

6 Heat the oven to 375°F. Bake the loaf in the heated oven until golden brown and the bread starts to shrink from the side of the mold, 40–45 minutes. Let cool slightly on the wire rack, then carefully unmold.

Chives add specks of color and flavor to bread

🍴 **TO SERVE**
With your fingers or 2 forks, pull the bread apart while still warm. It is delicious with roasted chicken.

Monkey bread pulls apart into rolls

SOUR CREAM AND DILL BREAD

Here, potato bread is flavored with sour cream and fresh dill.

1 Omit the melted butter for coating, and omit the chives. Strip the leaves from 5–7 sprigs of fresh dill, and coarsely chop them.
2 Prepare the potatoes and make the dough, using ¼ cup butter and adding the dill in place of the chives. Knead the dough, and let rise as directed in the main recipe.
3 Brush a ring mold with melted butter. Put ⅓ cup sour cream into a small bowl in place of the melted butter for coating. Knock the air out of the dough, and let rest as directed. Cut the dough in half. With your hands, shape 1 piece of dough into a cylinder about 2 inches in diameter. Cut the cylinder into 4 equal pieces. Repeat with the remaining dough.
4 Lightly flour the work surface. Cup a piece of dough under the palm of your hand and roll the dough in a circular motion so it forms a smooth ball. Drop the ball of dough into the prepared mold. With a pastry brush, brush the sides and top of the ball of dough generously with the sour cream. Repeat to shape and glaze the remaining dough, arranging the balls evenly around the mold.
5 Cover the loaf, and let rise as directed. Heat the oven to 375°F. Bake, cool, and unmold the bread as directed.

SESAME BREADSTICKS

Grissini Siciliani

EQUIPMENT

rolling pin

3 baking sheets

bowls

wire rack

dish towels

chef's knife

pastry brush

pastry scraper

INGREDIENTS

olive oil

sesame seeds

active dry yeast

unbleached all-purpose flour

sugar

Tradition has it that breadsticks should be pulled to the length of the baker's outstretched arms, though these sticks are a bit shorter than that. In the Sicilian style, sesame seeds are sprinkled on top.

GETTING AHEAD

Breadsticks can be kept up to 1 week in an airtight container.

*plus 1–1¹/₂ hours rising time

SHOPPING LIST

2 ¹/₂ tsp	active dry yeast, or ¹/₂ oz compressed yeast
1 ¹/₄ cups	lukewarm water
3 ¹/₂ cups	unbleached all-purpose flour, more if needed
1 tbsp	sugar
2 tsp	salt
2 tbsp	olive oil, more for brushing dough and baking sheets
¹/₃ cup	sesame seeds

ANNE SAYS
"You can make and knead the dough in a heavy-duty electric mixer fitted with a dough hook, or in a food processor."

ORDER OF WORK

1 MAKE, KNEAD, AND LET THE DOUGH RISE

2 CUT AND BAKE THE BREADSTICKS

1 MAKE, KNEAD, AND LET THE DOUGH RISE

1 In a small bowl, sprinkle or crumble the yeast over 1/2 cup of the water. Let stand until dissolved, stirring once, about 5 minutes.

Wall of flour should be uniform in thickness

Well made in center holds liquid ingredients

2 Put the flour onto a work surface with the sugar and salt. Make a large well in the center and add the dissolved yeast, remaining water, and the oil.

3 With your fingertips, work the ingredients in the well until thoroughly mixed. Begin to draw in the flour.

4 Continue to draw in the flour with the pastry scraper and work it into the other ingredients with your hand to form a smooth dough. It should be soft and slightly sticky.

5 Sprinkle the dough and your hands with flour, and begin to knead by holding the dough with one hand and pushing it away from you with the other.

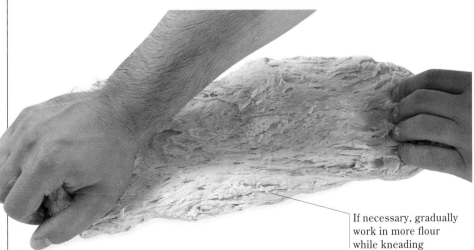

If necessary, gradually work in more flour while kneading

ANNE SAYS
"*Kneading is easy and more effective when you develop a regular, rhythmic action for pushing, peeling back, and turning the dough.*"

6 Continue to knead by peeling the dough from the surface. Give the dough a quarter turn, and knead until it is very smooth, elastic, and forms a ball, 5–7 minutes. If the dough sticks while kneading, flour the work surface.

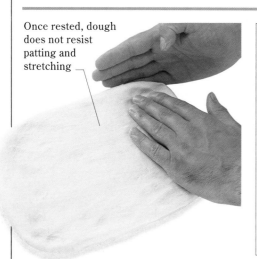

Once rested, dough does not resist patting and stretching

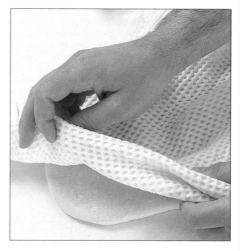

7 Cover the dough with a damp dish towel, and let rest, about 5 minutes. Flour your hands and pat the dough into a rectangle on a well-floured work surface.

8 With the rolling pin, roll the dough to a 16-x6-inch rectangle, pressing evenly so the breadsticks will be uniform in thickness. Brush the dough lightly with oil.

9 Cover the dough with the damp dish towel, and let rise until doubled in bulk, 1–1 1/2 hours. Rising time will depend on the temperature of the room.

2 CUT AND BAKE THE BREADSTICKS

1 Heat the oven to 425°F. Brush the baking sheets with oil. Gently lift the dough to prevent it sticking to the work surface. Lightly brush the dough with water.

2 Sprinkle the dough with the sesame seeds, and press them down gently into the dough.

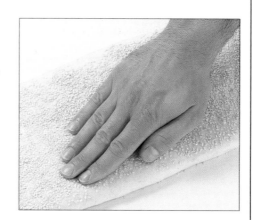

3 With the chef's knife, cut the dough across into 32 strips, each about 1/2-inch wide.

Use whole length of knife blade to cut dough

ANNE SAYS
"The dough is not left to rise after the breadsticks are cut."

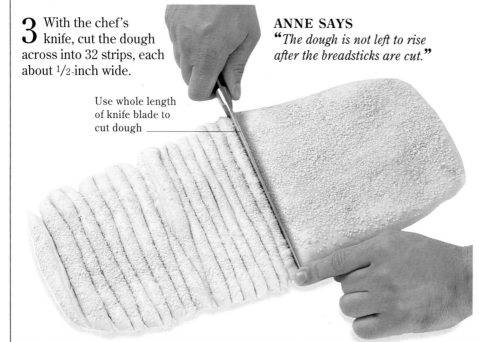

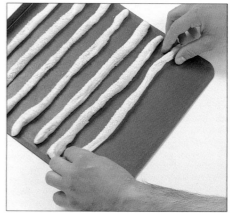

4 Stretch 1 strip of dough to the width of a baking sheet. Set it on 1 of the prepared baking sheets, letting the dough come just to the edges. Repeat to stretch the remaining strips, arranging them 3/4 inch apart on the baking sheets.

V A R I A T I O N

SPANISH BREAD LOOPS

Known as picos, *these crisp treats are made by tying strips of dough in loops. Coarse salt is sprinkled on top for flavor. The bread loops can be kept up to 1 week in an airtight container.*

1 Omit the sesame seeds. Make half of the dough, using $1\frac{1}{4}$ tsp active dry yeast, or $\frac{1}{4}$ oz compressed yeast, $\frac{2}{3}$ cup lukewarm water, $1\frac{3}{4}$ cups unbleached all-purpose flour, $1\frac{1}{2}$ tsp sugar, $\frac{1}{2}$ tsp salt, and 1 tbsp olive oil. Knead the dough, and let rest as directed. Roll the dough to an 8-x6-inch rectangle. Cover the dough, and let rise as directed.
2 Heat the oven to 425°F. Brush 2 baking sheets with oil. Cut the dough across into 16 strips, then cut each dough strip in half.

3 Loop each strip, twisting the ends in a single knot. Transfer to a prepared baking sheet, and repeat to shape the remaining strips.
4 Lightly brush the loops with water and sprinkle with $1\frac{1}{2}$ tbsp coarse salt. Bake the loops until golden and crisp, 18–20 minutes. Let the loops cool as directed.

5 Bake the breadsticks in the heated oven, 2 baking sheets at a time, until golden and crisp, 15–18 minutes. Transfer the breadsticks to the wire rack and let cool completely.

ANNE SAYS
"Keep the third sheet of unbaked breadsticks in the refrigerator until there is room to bake them in the oven."

🍽 **TO SERVE**
Serve breadsticks with cold and warm antipasti, or salad greens and cheese.

Breadsticks are
crisp and crunchy

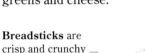

Sesame seeds
are savory
garnish for
breadsticks

PESTO GARLAND BREAD

🍴 MAKES 1 MEDIUM LOAF 🥣 WORK TIME 35–40 MINUTES* ☕ BAKING TIME 30–35 MINUTES

EQUIPMENT

food processor †

bowls

paper towels

wire rack   pastry brush

rubber spatula

chef's knife   pepper mill

rolling pin

baking sheet

dish towels

chopping board

†blender can also be used for
making pesto

To make this attractive loaf, a rye-flavored dough is spread with a fragrant pesto of basil, pine nuts, garlic, and Parmesan cheese. It is rolled into a cylinder, then slashed before baking to reveal spirals of filling.

GETTING AHEAD
This bread is best fresh, but it can be baked 1 day ahead and the flavor will mellow. Store it wrapped in foil, then warm it in a low oven before serving.
*plus 1 3/4–2 1/4 hours rising time

SHOPPING LIST

2 1/2 tsp	active dry yeast, or 1/2 oz compressed yeast
1 1/4 cups	lukewarm water
1 cup	rye flour
2 1/2 cups	unbleached all-purpose flour, more if needed
2 tsp	salt
	olive oil for bowl, baking sheet, and glaze
	For the filling
1/4 cup	pine nuts
3	garlic cloves
1	large bunch of fresh basil
3 tbsp	olive oil
1/2 cup	freshly grated Parmesan cheese
	freshly ground black pepper

INGREDIENTS

pine nuts

fresh basil

garlic cloves

black peppercorns

Parmesan cheese

active dry yeast

rye flour

unbleached all-purpose flour

olive oil

ANNE SAYS
"To save time, you can use 3/4 cup ready-prepared pesto."

ORDER OF WORK

1 MAKE, KNEAD, AND LET THE DOUGH RISE; MAKE THE PESTO

2 SHAPE AND BAKE THE LOAF

1 MAKE, KNEAD, AND LET THE DOUGH RISE; MAKE THE PESTO

1 Make and knead the dough in the food processor (see box, page 64).

ANNE SAYS
"If you like, you can make and knead the dough by hand. Start with the liquid ingredients in a large bowl, then add the dry ingredients."

2 Brush a large bowl with oil. Put the dough in the bowl, and flip it so it is lightly oiled. Cover the bowl with a damp dish towel and let the dough rise in a warm place until doubled in bulk, 1–1 1/2 hours.

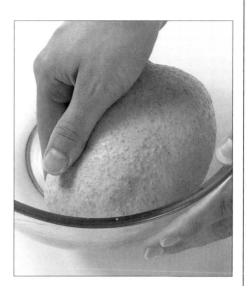

3 With the chef's knife, coarsely chop the pine nuts. Set the flat side of the chef's knife on top of each garlic clove and strike it with your fist. Discard the skin.

ANNE SAYS
"Garlic cloves are crushed to remove skin easily."

Weight and width of knife blade makes crushing garlic easy

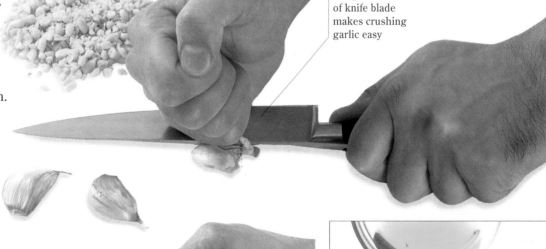

4 Strip the basil leaves from the stems. Rinse the leaves, dry them on paper towels, and put them in the food processor or blender with the garlic cloves.

Basil leaves must be dry so pesto is not watery

Pungent garlic and aromatic basil form base of pesto

5 Work the mixture until coarsely chopped. With the blades turning, gradually add the olive oil and work until smooth. Scrape down the side of the bowl from time to time with the rubber spatula.

HOW TO MAKE AND KNEAD DOUGH IN A FOOD PROCESSOR

The food processor is a fast alternative to making and kneading dough by hand. Standard food processors fitted with a steel blade are suitable for kneading doughs made with no more than 3 1/2 cups flour, therefore the processor is suggested for small quantities only. If you have a large machine, you may use the plastic dough blade to knead larger quantities.

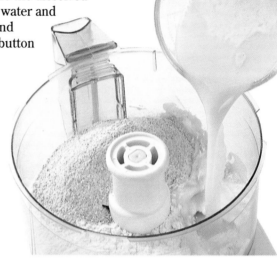

2 Put the rye flour and half of the all-purpose flour in the work bowl with the salt. Combine the dissolved yeast and remaining water and pour into the bowl, and work with the pulse button just until mixed.

ANNE SAYS
"This dough-making method can be used in a variety of recipes, using dry and liquid ingredients as specified."

1 In a small bowl, sprinkle or crumble the yeast over 1/4 cup of the water. Let stand until dissolved, stirring once, about 5 minutes.

3 Add the remaining flour, 1/2 cup at a time. Work each addition with the pulse button just until mixed. Keep adding flour until the dough starts to pull away from the side of the bowl in a ball. It should be soft and slightly sticky.

Work in each batch of flour before adding more

4 Continue working the dough in the food processor until it is very smooth and elastic, 60 seconds longer. Turn the dough onto a lightly floured work surface and remove the blade. Shape the dough into a ball.

! TAKE CARE !
If the food processor slows down and the motor begins to strain, turn it off. Continue kneading the dough by hand.

Pesto ingredients come together easily

Pine nuts add texture to mixture

6 Transfer the pesto mixture to a bowl and stir in the pine nuts, Parmesan cheese, and plenty of black pepper. Taste for seasoning.

! TAKE CARE !
The Parmesan cheese is salty, so you may not need any salt.

2 SHAPE AND BAKE THE LOAF

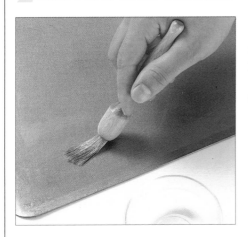

1 Brush the baking sheet with oil. Turn the dough onto a lightly floured work surface and knead with your hand just to knock out the air, 15–20 seconds. Cover the dough, and let rest, about 5 minutes.

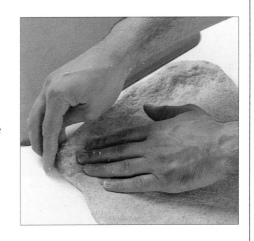

2 Flatten the dough with the palms of your hands, then roll it into a 16-x 12-inch rectangle with the rolling pin. If necessary, use your hands to shape the rectangle.

Apply gentle pressure with spatula to spread pesto evenly

3 With the rubber spatula, spread the pesto filling evenly over the dough, leaving a ¹/₂-inch border.

Border is left so dough rolls into cylinder easily

4 Starting with a long end, roll up the rectangle into a cylinder, keeping the cylinder even from middle to end.

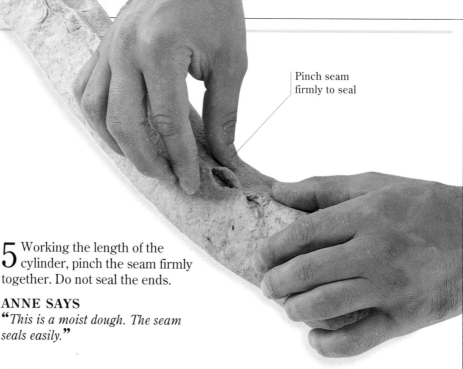

Pinch seam firmly to seal

5 Working the length of the cylinder, pinch the seam firmly together. Do not seal the ends.

ANNE SAYS
"This is a moist dough. The seam seals easily."

Center ring on baking sheet

Press and pinch ends together to seal ring

6 Transfer the cylinder seam-side down to the prepared baking sheet. Curve the cylinder into a ring, overlapping and sealing the ends.

7 With the chef's knife, make a series of deep cuts around the ring, about 2 inches apart.

! TAKE CARE !
Do not cut completely through the ring.

8 Pull the slices apart slightly and twist them over to lie flat. Cover with a dry dish towel and let the loaf rise in a warm place until doubled in bulk, about 45 minutes.

9 Heat the oven to 425°F. Brush the loaf with oil and bake in the heated oven, 10 minutes. Reduce the heat to 375°F and continue baking until well browned, 20–25 minutes longer.

10 Carefully transfer the bread from the baking sheet to the wire rack and let cool slightly.

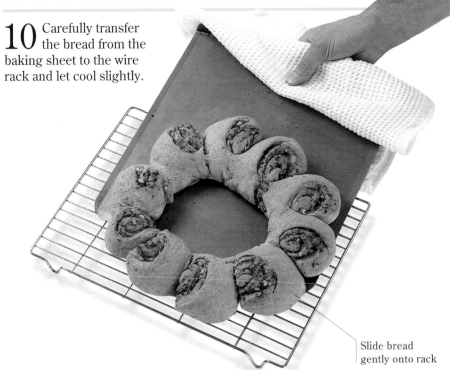

Slide bread gently onto rack

SUN-DRIED TOMATO SPIRAL

Sun-dried tomatoes make a gutsy filling for this spiral loaf.

🍽 TO SERVE
Serve this bread as an accompaniment to pasta or a salad of ripe tomatoes.

Spirals expose savory filling

Garland is sliced or broken into pieces

1 Make, knead, and let the dough rise.
2 Drain 1/3 cup oil-packed sun-dried tomatoes, reserving 2 tbsp of the oil, and coarsely chop them. Chop the pine nuts. Peel and chop 2 garlic cloves. Strip the leaves from 5–10 sprigs of fresh basil and finely chop them.
3 Put the sun-dried tomatoes in a small bowl with the pine nuts, garlic, basil, and 1/2 cup grated Parmesan cheese. Stir in 1 tbsp reserved oil and season with plenty of black pepper.
4 Brush an 8-inch round cake pan with the remaining oil. Sprinkle 1–2 tbsp cornmeal in the pan and turn it to coat the bottom and side; turn the pan upside down and tap to remove excess cornmeal. Knock the air out of the dough and let rest as directed. Roll the dough into a rectangle, spread with filling, and shape a cylinder.
5 Flip the cylinder over so the seam-side is down, then curve it around into a spiral, tucking the end underneath. Drop the spiral into the pan, cover, and let rise as directed. Bake the loaf as directed, allowing 25–30 minutes at 375°F. Unmold and let cool.

SPICED LAMB PIES

 MAKES 12   WORK TIME 40–45 MINUTES*   BAKING TIME 10–15 MINUTES

EQUIPMENT

chef's knife

pastry brush

small knife

large sauté pan
with lid†

saucepan

bowls

dish towels   2 baking sheets

chopping board

wooden spoon

slotted spoon

rolling pin

†frying pan can also be used

ANNE SAYS
*"You can make and knead
the dough in a heavy-duty
electric mixer fitted with
a dough hook, or in a food
processor."*

*Here, a slightly leavened dough is shaped around
a spicy lamb filling to form triangular pies
reminiscent of those found in the Middle East.*

GETTING AHEAD
The filling can be prepared and refrigerated up to 1 day
ahead. Make the dough, shape, and bake the pies
just before serving.
plus 1 1/2–1 3/4 hours rising time

SHOPPING LIST

1 tsp	active dry yeast, or 1/5 oz compressed yeast
1 cup	lukewarm water
2 tsp	olive oil, more for bowl and baking sheets
1 tsp	salt
1/2 cup	whole wheat flour
2 cups	unbleached all-purpose flour, more if needed
	For the filling
3	large garlic cloves
5–7	sprigs of fresh coriander (cilantro)
1/2-inch	piece of fresh ginger root
1	medium onion
2	medium tomatoes
2 tbsp	olive oil
3/4 lb	ground lamb
	pepper
1/2 tsp	ground coriander
1/4 tsp	ground cumin
1/4 tsp	ground turmeric
1	large pinch of cayenne pepper

INGREDIENTS

fresh ginger root   ground lamb

tomatoes

unbleached
all-purpose flour

olive oil   whole wheat flour

onion   garlic
cloves

ground
coriander   cayenne pepper

ground cumin   ground turmeric

active dry yeast

fresh coriander

ORDER OF WORK

1 MAKE, KNEAD,
AND LET THE
DOUGH RISE

2 PREPARE THE
FILLING

3 SHAPE AND BAKE
THE PIES

1 MAKE, KNEAD, AND LET THE DOUGH RISE

1 In a small bowl, sprinkle or crumble the yeast over ¼ cup of the water. Let stand until dissolved, stirring once, about 5 minutes.

2 Put the dissolved yeast, remaining water, oil, and salt in a large bowl. Stir in the whole wheat flour with half of the all-purpose flour and mix well with your hand.

3 Add the remaining all-purpose flour, ½ cup at a time, mixing well after each addition. Keep adding flour until the dough pulls away from the side of the bowl in a ball. It should be soft and slightly sticky. Turn the dough onto a floured work surface, and knead by hand (see box, below).

HOW TO KNEAD DOUGH BY HAND

Kneading is important in bread making because it distributes the yeast, and develops the gluten. Gluten holds the gas bubbles produced by the yeast and gives elasticity to bread dough. Sufficient kneading gives bread an even texture. The amount of flour the dough absorbs while kneading and kneading time vary with each recipe.

1 Holding the dough with one hand, press firmly down into the dough with the heel of your other hand, pushing the dough away from you.

2 Peel the dough back from the work surface in one piece, fold it over, and give it a quarter turn.

Hands and work surface should be lightly floured

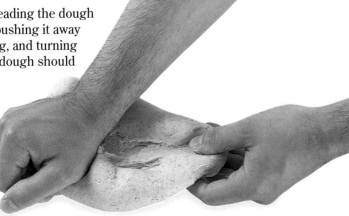

3 Continue kneading the dough in this way, pushing it away from you, peeling, and turning it. The kneaded dough should be very smooth, elastic, and in the form of a ball. If the dough sticks while kneading, flour the work surface.

4 Press the dough with your finger. The dough will spring back when it has been sufficiently kneaded.

Roll dough against side of bowl to coat lightly in oil

4 Wash the large bowl and brush it with oil. Put the kneaded dough in the bowl, and flip it so the surface is lightly oiled. Cover the bowl with a damp dish towel and let the dough rise in a warm place until doubled in bulk, 1–1½ hours. Prepare the filling.

ANNE SAYS
"The speed at which the dough rises depends largely on its temperature – the warmer it is, the quicker it rises."

2 PREPARE THE FILLING

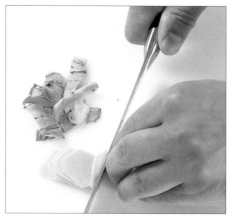

1 Set the flat side of the chef's knife on top of each garlic clove and strike it with your fist. Discard the skin and finely chop the cloves.

2 Strip the coriander leaves from the stems and pile them on the chopping board. With the chef's knife, finely chop the leaves.

3 With the small knife, peel the skin from the ginger root. With the chef's knife, slice the ginger, cutting across the fibrous grain. Crush each slice with the flat of the knife, then finely chop the slices.

ANNE SAYS
"Mature ginger is usually peeled before use. Young ginger, pink in color and less pungent in flavor, does not have a tough skin and can be used without peeling."

Classic onion chopping technique produces uniform dice

Use knuckles to guide knife

4 Peel the onion, leaving a little of the root attached, and cut it lengthwise in half. Lay each onion half flat on the chopping board and slice horizontally toward the root, leaving the slices attached at the root end. Then slice vertically, again leaving the root end uncut. Finally, cut across the onion to make dice.

Tomatoes are scored before blanching to make peeling easy

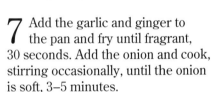

5 Cut out the cores, and score an "x" on the base of each tomato. Immerse the tomatoes in a saucepan of boiling water until the skins start to split, 8–15 seconds, depending on their ripeness. With the slotted spoon, transfer the tomatoes at once to a bowl of cold water. When cool, peel off the skins. Cut the tomatoes crosswise in half, squeeze out the seeds, then coarsely chop each half.

6 Heat the oil in the sauté pan. Add the lamb, season with salt and pepper, and cook over medium-high heat, stirring often to break up the meat, until it is evenly browned, 5–7 minutes. With the slotted spoon, transfer the lamb to a bowl. Reduce the heat to medium and pour off all but 2 tbsp of the fat.

7 Add the garlic and ginger to the pan and fry until fragrant, 30 seconds. Add the onion and cook, stirring occasionally, until the onion is soft, 3–5 minutes.

8 Add the ground coriander, cumin, turmeric, and cayenne pepper to the pan. Add the lamb and the tomatoes, cover and cook, stirring occasionally, until thickened, about 10 minutes.

Fresh coriander is added at end of cooking to preserve its delicate flavor

9 Remove the pan from the heat. Stir in the chopped coriander and taste for seasoning. Let the filling cool.

ANNE SAYS
"Taste the lamb mixture again once it has cooled. It should be well seasoned."

Lamb filling is aromatic with spices

2 SHAPE AND BAKE THE PIES

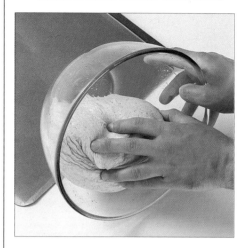

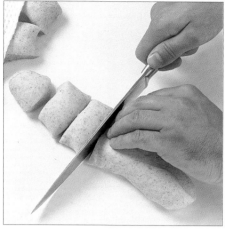

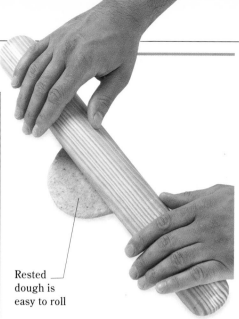

Rested dough is easy to roll

1 Brush the baking sheets with oil. Turn the dough onto a lightly floured work surface and knead with your hand just to knock out the air, 15–20 seconds. Cover the dough, and let rest, about 5 minutes.

2 Cut the dough in half. With your hands, roll 1 piece of dough into a cylinder about 2 inches in diameter. Cut the cylinder into 6 pieces, and cover them. Repeat to shape and divide the remaining dough.

3 Shape a piece of dough into a ball. With the rolling pin, roll the ball into a 4-inch round.

ANNE SAYS
"Be sure to keep work surface lightly floured."

Lamb mixture is studded with onion and tomato

5 With your fingers, lift the dough up and over the lamb filling to form a triangular parcel.

Use 1–2 tbsp of lamb mixture to fill each pie

4 Spoon some of the lamb filling into the center of the round, leaving a 1-inch border of dough.

! TAKE CARE !
Work quickly to keep dough from drying out.

6 Pinch the edges together with your fingers to seal. Place the pie on a prepared baking sheet. Repeat to shape and fill the remaining dough.

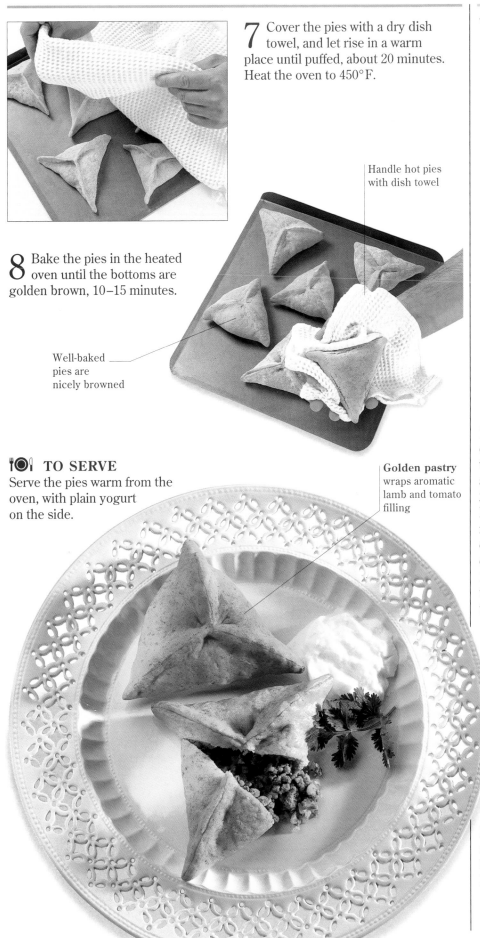

7 Cover the pies with a dry dish towel, and let rise in a warm place until puffed, about 20 minutes. Heat the oven to 450°F.

Handle hot pies with dish towel

8 Bake the pies in the heated oven until the bottoms are golden brown, 10–15 minutes.

Well-baked pies are nicely browned

🍽 **TO SERVE**
Serve the pies warm from the oven, with plain yogurt on the side.

Golden pastry wraps aromatic lamb and tomato filling

VARIATION

PITA BREAD

This pocket bread is delicious completely plain or stuffed with salad. I sometimes add cumin seeds to the dough, as suggested here.

1 Omit the lamb filling. Make the dough, adding 2 tsp cumin seeds with the flour. Knead the dough, and let rise as directed.

2 Generously flour 2 baking sheets. Knock the air out of the dough and let rest as directed. Roll the dough into a cylinder about 2 inches wide, then cut the cylinder into 6 pieces. Shape 1 piece of dough into a ball, then roll the ball into a 7-inch round. Transfer the round to a prepared baking sheet. Repeat to shape the remaining dough. Cover the dough, and let rise as directed.

3 Heat the oven to 500°F. Put an additional baking sheet in the oven to heat. With a metal spatula, gently loosen the rounds from 1 of the baking sheets. Slide the loosened rounds all at once onto the heated baking sheet and bake them in the oven until puffed, about 5 minutes.

4 Transfer the breads to a wire rack and brush the tops lightly with water. Bake the remaining rounds. Brush any excess flour off the bottom of each bread and serve while still warm. Makes 6 pita breads.

CORNMEAL PIZZAS WITH ONION CONFIT AND GORGONZOLA

 MAKES 6   WORK TIME 40–45 MINUTES*   BAKING TIME 15–20 MINUTES

EQUIPMENT

wooden spoon

chef's knife

pastry brush

medium frying pan with lid

dish towels

pastry scraper

bowls

chopping board

aluminum foil

rolling pin

2 baking sheets

ANNE SAYS
"You can make and knead the dough in a heavy-duty electric mixer fitted with a dough hook, or in a food processor."

Onion and Gorgonzola cheese make a delicious combination, here topping a crust made crunchy by the addition of cornmeal. To make confit, sliced red onions are cooked very slowly to soften in their own juices, with a little red wine added for color.

GETTING AHEAD
The onion confit can be made 1 day ahead and kept, covered, in the refrigerator. The pizza dough can be made, kneaded, and left in the refrigerator to rise overnight. Shape the dough and let it come to room temperature. Assemble and bake the pizzas just before serving.
plus 1 1/4 – 1 3/4 hours rising time

SHOPPING LIST

1 1/2 tsp	active dry yeast, or 1/3 oz compressed yeast
1 cup	lukewarm water
2 cups	unbleached all-purpose flour, more if needed
1/2 cup	yellow cornmeal, more for squares of foil
1 tsp	salt
2 tbsp	olive oil, more for bowl and serving
	For the topping
1 1/2 lb	red onions
2 tbsp	olive oil
2 tsp	sugar
	pepper
1/4 cup	red wine
5–7	sprigs of fresh oregano
6 oz	Gorgonzola cheese

INGREDIENTS

red onions

Gorgonzola cheese†

red wine

olive oil

active dry yeast

yellow cornmeal

fresh oregano

unbleached all-purpose flour

sugar

†Roquefort cheese can also be used

ORDER OF WORK

1 MAKE, KNEAD, AND LET THE DOUGH RISE

2 MAKE THE ONION CONFIT

3 ASSEMBLE AND BAKE THE PIZZAS

1 MAKE, KNEAD, AND LET THE DOUGH RISE

1 In a small bowl, sprinkle or crumble the yeast over ¼ cup of the water. Let stand until dissolved, stirring once, about 5 minutes.

2 Put the flour onto the work surface with the cornmeal and salt. Make a large well in the center and add the remaining water, the oil, and dissolved yeast.

3 With your fingertips, work the ingredients in the well until thoroughly mixed. Begin to draw in the flour.

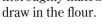
Draw flour into liquid ingredients without breaking through side of well

4 Continue to draw in flour with the pastry scraper and work it into the other ingredients with your hand to form a smooth dough. It should be soft and slightly sticky.

ANNE SAYS
"If necessary, work in more flour while kneading the dough."

5 Sprinkle the dough and your hands with flour, and begin to knead by holding the dough with one hand and pushing it away from you with the other.

ANNE SAYS
"Kneading is easy and more effective when you develop a regular, rhythmic action for pushing, peeling back, and turning the dough."

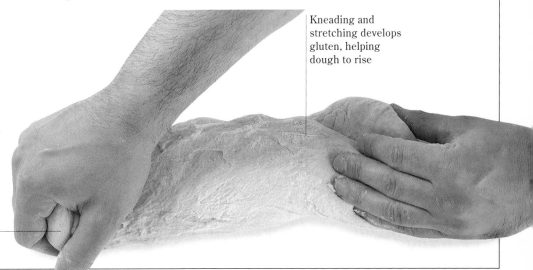

Kneading and stretching develops gluten, helping dough to rise

Push dough firmly against floured work surface

6 Continue to knead by peeling the dough from the surface. Give the dough a quarter turn, and knead until it is very smooth, elastic, and forms a ball, 5–7 minutes. If the dough sticks while kneading, flour the work surface.

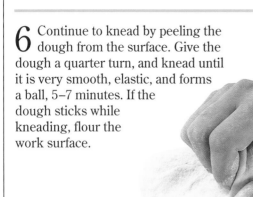

Dough becomes very smooth during kneading

7 Let the dough rise in a warm place until doubled in bulk (see box, below), 1–1½ hours. Meanwhile, prepare the onion confit.

HOW TO LET DOUGH RISE

Once activated, yeast grows, causing dough to rise. The speed at which dough rises is largely controlled by temperature. In a warm place, such as an oven warmed just by the pilot light, or an electric oven with the oven light turned on, dough rises quickly. At room temperature, or in a refrigerator, dough rises at a slower rate. Dough is normally left to rise twice, after kneading, and after it has been shaped. The flavor of the dough also develops as it rises. Rising time varies with the type of dough, and is indicated in each recipe.

1 Brush a large bowl with oil or melted butter.

2 Put the kneaded dough in the bowl, and flip it so its surface is covered lightly with the oil or butter.

4 To test the dough, press it gently, but firmly, with your forefinger. If the dough holds the impression of your finger, it has risen sufficiently.

! TAKE CARE !
When dough is left to rise too long, bubbles start to break on the surface, causing its eventual collapse.

3 To prevent the dough from drying out, cover the bowl with a damp dish towel, or with plastic wrap, and let it rise in a warm place, about 85°F, until doubled in bulk.

Risen dough holds impression of forefinger

2 MAKE THE ONION CONFIT

Use knuckles to guide knife

1 Peel the onions, leaving a little of the root attached, then cut them lengthwise in half. Lay each onion half flat on a chopping board and cut across into thin, even slices.

2 Heat the oil in the frying pan. Add the onions, sugar, salt, and pepper. Cook over medium heat, stirring often, until the onions are soft and lightly brown, 5–7 minutes.

3 Add the wine to the onions and continue cooking until the wine has evaporated, 1–2 minutes longer. Lower the heat, press a piece of foil on top of the onions, and cover with the pan lid.

4 Cook the onions over very low heat, stirring occasionally, until they are soft enough to cut with a spoon, 15–20 minutes. Let cool.

Rock chef's knife from tip to heel of blade to chop herbs efficiently

Sharp chef's knife makes easy work of chopping herbs

5 Strip the oregano leaves from the stems, reserving 6 sprigs for decoration. Pile the leaves on the chopping board and finely chop them with the chef's knife. Stir the chopped oregano into the onion confit.

ANNE SAYS
"Choose your favorite herb; fresh basil, sage, thyme, or marjoram all work well here."

3 ASSEMBLE AND BAKE THE PIZZAS

1 Heat the oven to 450°F. Put the baking sheets on separate racks in the bottom half of the oven to heat. Cut six 9-inch squares of foil, and sprinkle each generously with cornmeal.

2 Turn the dough onto a lightly floured work surface and knead with your hand to knock out the air, 15–20 seconds. Cover the dough, and let rest, about 5 minutes.

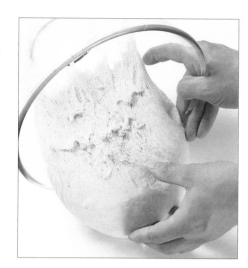

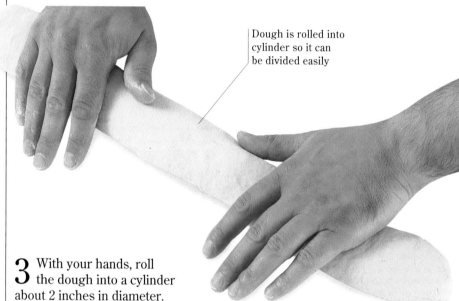

Dough is rolled into cylinder so it can be divided easily

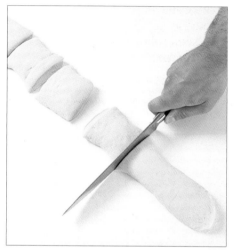

3 With your hands, roll the dough into a cylinder about 2 inches in diameter.

4 With the chef's knife, cut the cylinder in half, and then cut each half into 3 equal pieces.

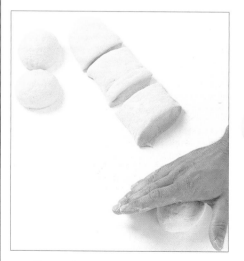

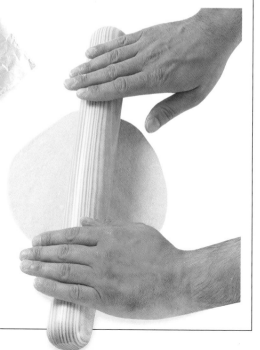

5 Shape the pieces of dough into balls: cup a piece of dough under the palm of your hand, and roll it in a circular motion.

6 Roll a ball of dough into a 7-inch round. Transfer the round to 1 of the squares of prepared foil. Repeat to shape the remaining balls of dough.

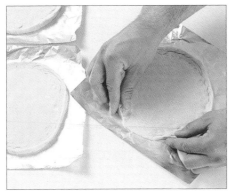

7 Press up the edges of the rounds with your fingertips to form shallow rims. Spread the rounds with the onion confit.

8 Top the rounds with cheese, and let rise in a warm place until the dough is puffed, about 15 minutes. Bake the pizzas, on the foil, on the baking sheets, until lightly browned and crisp, 15–20 minutes. Switch the baking sheets after 7 minutes so the pizzas brown evenly.

ANNE SAYS
"*Baking the pizzas on a hot baking sheet makes for crisp crusts. Foil makes them easy to transfer.*"

Gorgonzola should be soft for crumbling

🍽 **TO SERVE**
Serve the pizzas hot from the oven. Brush the crust with olive oil, and top with the reserved oregano sprigs.

Crust brushed with olive oil is golden and flavorful

Pizza topping is mellow with caramelized onions and sharp with Gorgonzola cheese

CORNMEAL PIZZAS WITH RICOTTA AND SPINACH

Here, cornmeal pizzas are topped with ricotta cheese, sautéed spinach, and ripe plum tomatoes.

1 Omit the onions, sugar, red wine, oregano, and Gorgonzola. Make, knead, and let the dough rise as directed. Peel and chop 2 garlic cloves. Discard the tough ribs and stems from 1 1/2 lb spinach, then wash the leaves in plenty of cold water. Dry the spinach well. Roll a few spinach leaves and cut across into shreds. Shred the rest.
2 Heat 2 tbsp olive oil in a large frying pan. Add the garlic and fry until fragrant, 30 seconds. Add the spinach, salt, and pepper, and stir. Cover the pan and cook over medium-high heat until the spinach is wilted, 3–5 minutes. Uncover and cook, stirring constantly, until any moisture evaporates, 1–2 minutes longer. Taste for seasoning and let the spinach cool. Core 5 plum tomatoes, and cut each one lengthwise into 4 slices. Season 1 1/2 cups ricotta cheese with salt and pepper.
3 Heat the oven to 450°F, and heat 2 baking sheets as directed. Prepare the foil and shape the rounds as directed. Spread the cheese on the rounds, then top each with spinach, tomato slices, 1 tsp olive oil, and freshly ground black pepper. Let rise, then bake as directed.

CHICAGO DEEP-DISH PIZZA

🍽 SERVES 6–8   🥣 WORK TIME 35–40 MINUTES*   🍲 BAKING TIME 20–25 MINUTES

EQUIPMENT

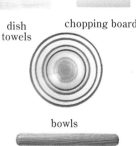

grater

14-inch deep-dish pizza pan†

small knife

chef's knife

pastry brush

medium sauté pan‡

slotted spoon

wooden spoon

medium saucepan

baking sheet

pastry scraper

dish towels

chopping board

bowls

rolling pin

†two 9-inch round cake pans can also be used

‡medium frying pan can also be used

Deep-dish pizza, with its hearty crust and topping, first made its appearance in Chicago in the 1940s. Here, mild Italian sausage flavors a simple sauce of fresh tomatoes, topped with mozzarella cheese.

GETTING AHEAD

The sauce can be made 1 day ahead and kept, covered, in the refrigerator. The pizza dough can be made, kneaded, and left in the refrigerator to rise overnight. Shape the dough and let it come to room temperature. Assemble and bake the pizza just before serving.

plus 1 1/2–2 hours rising time

SHOPPING LIST

2 1/2 tsp	active dry yeast, or 1/2 oz compressed yeast
1 1/2 cups	lukewarm water
4 cups	unbleached all-purpose flour, more if needed
2 tsp	salt
3 tbsp	olive oil, more for bowl and pizza pan
2–3 tbsp	yellow cornmeal
	For the sauce
2 lb	plum tomatoes
3	garlic cloves
7–10	sprigs of flat-leaf parsley
3/4 lb	mild Italian sausage
1 tbsp	olive oil
	pepper
6 oz	mozzarella cheese

INGREDIENTS

Italian sausage

garlic cloves

active dry yeast

plum tomatoes†

yellow cornmeal

unbleached all-purpose flour

mozzarella cheese

olive oil

flat-leaf parsley‡

†28 oz canned plum tomatoes, drained, can also be used

‡curly parsley can also be used

ANNE SAYS
"If you prefer a spicy topping, use hot Italian sausage."

ORDER OF WORK

1 MAKE, KNEAD, AND LET THE DOUGH RISE

2 MAKE THE PIZZA SAUCE

3 ASSEMBLE AND BAKE THE PIZZA

1 MAKE, KNEAD, AND LET THE DOUGH RISE

1 In a small bowl, sprinkle or crumble the yeast over 1/4 cup of the water. Let stand until dissolved, stirring once, about 5 minutes.

2 Put the flour onto a work surface with the salt. Make a large well in the center and add the dissolved yeast, remaining water, and the oil.

Wall of flour forms well for liquid ingredients

3 With your fingertips, work the liquid ingredients in the center of the well until thoroughly and evenly mixed. Begin to draw in the flour.

4 Continue to draw in the flour with the pastry scraper and work it into the other ingredients with your hand to form a smooth dough. It should be soft and slightly sticky.

Dough peels from surface in one piece

Kneading develops gluten, helping dough to rise

5 Sprinkle the dough and your hands with flour, and begin to knead by holding the dough with one hand and pushing it away from you with the other. Continue to knead by peeling the dough from the surface. Give the dough a quarter turn and knead until it is very smooth, elastic, and forms a ball, 5–7 minutes. If the dough sticks while kneading, flour the work surface.

ANNE SAYS
"You can make and knead the dough in a heavy-duty electric mixer fitted with a dough hook."

Olive oil keeps
dough moist
while it rises, and
imparts flavor

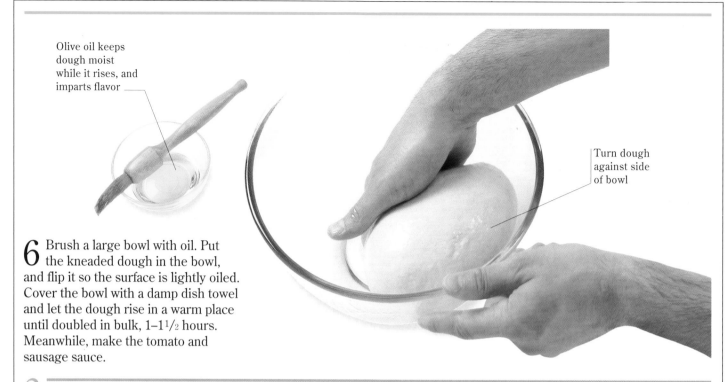

Turn dough
against side
of bowl

6 Brush a large bowl with oil. Put the kneaded dough in the bowl, and flip it so the surface is lightly oiled. Cover the bowl with a damp dish towel and let the dough rise in a warm place until doubled in bulk, 1–1½ hours. Meanwhile, make the tomato and sausage sauce.

2 MAKE THE PIZZA SAUCE

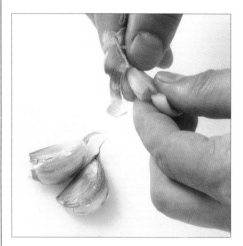

1 Peel, seed, and chop the tomatoes (see box, page 83). Set the flat side of the chef's knife on top of each garlic clove and strike it with your fist. Discard the skin and finely chop the cloves.

2 Wash and dry the parsley sprigs only if they are dirty. Strip the leaves from the stems and pile the leaves on the chopping board.

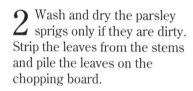

3 With the chef's knife, and using your knuckles as a guide, coarsely chop the parsley leaves.

Once out of
casing, sausage
meat breaks
up easily

Casing peels
easily from
sausage meat

4 Slit the side of each sausage and push out the meat, discarding the casing.

HOW TO PEEL, SEED, AND CHOP TOMATOES

Tomatoes are often peeled and seeded before chopping so they need not be strained after cooking. The technique is the same for any variety of tomato.

1 Cut the cores from the tomatoes and score an "x" on the base of each tomato with the tip of a small knife.

2 Immerse the tomatoes in a pan of boiling water until the skins start to split, 8–15 seconds depending on their ripeness. Transfer the tomatoes at once to a bowl of cold water.

3 When the tomatoes are cool enough to handle, peel the skin off each one, using the small knife.

4 With a chef's knife, cut the tomatoes crosswise in half. Squeeze out the seeds, then coarsely chop each tomato half.

Hold tip of blade and rock handle up and down

5 Heat the oil in the sauté pan. Add the sausage meat and fry over medium-high heat, breaking up the meat with the wooden spoon, until cooked, 5–7 minutes. Reduce the heat to medium, remove the sausage meat from the pan, and pour off all but 1 tbsp of the fat.

Stir sausage meat for even cooking

Fat is rendered as sausage meat cooks

Sausage, tomatoes, garlic, and parsley make savory and aromatic sauce

Some parsley is reserved for sprinkling on top of pizza

6 Stir the garlic into the pan and fry until fragrant, about 30 seconds. Add the sausage back to the pan, and stir in the tomatoes, salt, pepper, and all but 1 tbsp of the parsley.

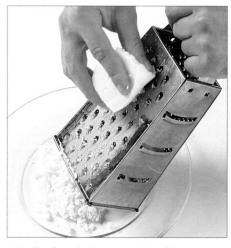

7 Cook, stirring occasionally, until the sauce is thickened, 10–15 minutes. Remove the sauce from the heat, taste for seasoning, and let cool completely. Coarsely grate the cheese.

3 ASSEMBLE AND BAKE THE PIZZA

1 Brush the pizza pan with oil. Sprinkle the cornmeal in the pan and turn it to coat the bottom and side; turn the pan upside down and tap to remove excess cornmeal.

2 Turn the dough onto a lightly floured work surface and knead with your hand just to knock out the air, 15–20 seconds. Cover, and let rest, about 5 minutes.

3 Shape the dough into a loose ball. With the rolling pin, roll the ball into a 14-inch round.

4 Working carefully, wrap the dough around the rolling pin and drape it over the pan.

5 With your hands, press the dough into the bottom of the pan, and 1 inch up the side to form a rim.

6 Cover the pan with a dry dish towel, and let the dough rise until slightly puffed, about 20 minutes. Heat the oven to 450°F. Heat a baking sheet in the bottom third of the oven.

Sprinkling of chopped parsley is more pronounced in flavor than parsley cooked in sauce

7 Spread the sauce over the the dough, leaving a 1/2-inch border around the edge. Sprinkle over the cheese and the remaining chopped parsley. Bake the pizza on the baking sheet in the bottom third of heated oven until the cheese is lightly browned and the dough is crisp and golden, 20–25 minutes.

🍴 TO SERVE

Deep-dish pizza is often served from the pizza pan, but it can be taken out for easy slicing. Let the pizza cool 5 minutes, then cut it into wedges.

Thick crust and hearty topping are signatures of deep-dish pizza

V A R I A T I O N

PIZZA CALABRESE

Here, pizza dough is stuffed with artichoke hearts, black olives, and capers to make savory pies.

1 Make, knead, and let the dough rise as directed. Omit the sausage and make the sauce, using all the parsley. Drain and slice 1 1/2 cups oil-packed artichoke hearts. Pit and chop 1/4 cup oil-cured black olives. Chop 2 tsp capers. Grate the cheese.
2 Prepare two 9-inch round cake pans as directed. Knead the dough just to knock out the air. Cut the dough into 3 equal pieces. Shape 1 piece into a ball, then roll it to an 11-inch round. Drape it over 1 of the prepared pans, allowing some dough to hang over the side, and pressing the dough into the bottom of the pan. Line the second pan.
3 Spread the sauce over the dough in each pan, then top with the vegetables and cheese. Cut the remaining piece of dough in half. Roll each half to an 8-inch round. Drape the rounds over the filling, leaving a 1-inch border. Brush a 1/2-inch border of water around the edge of each round. Lift the bottom rounds of dough over the filling just to meet the top rounds, pressing gently to seal.
4 Let rise as directed. Brush the dough with olive oil, and cut an "x" in the center of each pie. Bake the pies and let cool as directed. Makes 2 pies.

FOCACCIA WITH ROSEMARY

EQUIPMENT

wire rack

dish towels

15- x 9-inch
jelly roll pan

bowls

chef's knife

pastry scraper

pepper mill

pastry brush

chopping board

This moist Italian flat bread has many interpretations. Its shape, and the ingredients with which it is flavored, differ from region to region. It can be sweet or savory, is most often baked, but sometimes fried. Here it is at its simplest and best – flavored with fresh rosemary, black pepper, and olive oil.

GETTING AHEAD

Focaccia is best freshly baked and hot from the oven. The dough can be made, kneaded, and left in the refrigerator to rise overnight. Shape the dough, let it come to room temperature, then bake as directed.

*plus 1 1/2–2 1/4 hours rising time

INGREDIENTS

black peppercorns

fresh rosemary

unbleached all-purpose flour

olive oil

active dry yeast

ORDER OF WORK

1 MAKE, KNEAD, AND LET THE DOUGH RISE

2 SHAPE AND BAKE THE FOCACCIA

ANNE SAYS

"You can make and knead the dough in a heavy-duty electric mixer fitted with a dough hook, or in a food processor."

SHOPPING LIST

5–7	sprigs of fresh rosemary
1 tbsp	active dry yeast, or 2/3 oz compressed yeast
1 1/4 cups	lukewarm water
3 1/2 cups	unbleached all-purpose flour, more if needed
2 tsp	salt
6 tbsp	olive oil, more for bowl and jelly roll pan
1/4 tsp	freshly ground black pepper

1 MAKE, KNEAD, AND LET THE DOUGH RISE

Finely chop rosemary; leaves can be tough

1 Strip the rosemary leaves from the stems and pile two-thirds of the leaves on the chopping board. With the chef's knife, finely chop them. Reserve the remaining whole rosemary leaves for topping the focaccia.

2 In a small bowl, sprinkle or crumble the yeast over ¼ cup of the water. Let stand until dissolved, stirring once, about 5 minutes.

Liquid ingredients are combined before working in flour

Keep wall of flour intact while combining liquid ingredients

3 Put the flour onto the work surface with the salt. Make a large well in the center and add the chopped rosemary, dissolved yeast, ¼ cup of the oil, the freshly ground pepper, and the remaining water.

4 With your fingertips, work the ingredients in the well until thoroughly mixed.

5 Gradually draw in the flour with the pastry scraper and work it into the other ingredients with your hand to form a smooth dough. It should be soft and sticky.

! TAKE CARE !
The dough should be quite sticky so add as little flour as possible when kneading.

6 Sprinkle the dough and your hands with flour and knead, lifting the dough up and throwing it down until it is very smooth, elastic, and forms a ball, 5–7 minutes.

Only a thin
coating of oil
is needed

7 Cover the dough with a dish towel, and brush a large bowl with olive oil.

8 Put the kneaded dough in the bowl, and flip it so the surface is lightly oiled. Cover the bowl with a damp dish towel and let the dough rise in a warm place until doubled in bulk, 1–1¹/₂ hours.

2 SHAPE AND BAKE THE FOCACCIA

1 Once the dough has doubled in bulk, generously brush the jelly roll pan with olive oil.

2 Turn the dough onto a lightly floured work surface and knead with your hand just to knock out the air, 15–20 seconds. Cover the dough and let rest, about 5 minutes.

3 Transfer the dough to the pan. With your hands, flatten the dough to fill the pan evenly. Cover the dough with a dry dish towel, and let rise in a warm place until puffed, 35–45 minutes.

Rosemary is traditional focaccia garnish

4 Heat the oven to 400°F. Brush the dough with the remaining oil, then top with the reserved rosemary leaves.

5 With your fingertips, poke the dough all over to make deep dimples.

Press down through dough to pan to make deep dimples

Focaccia slides easily from pan to wire rack

6 Bake the focaccia in the heated oven until crisp-crusted underneath and lightly browned on top, 15–20 minutes. Transfer the bread to the wire rack and let cool slightly.

🍴 **TO SERVE**
Cut or break the focaccia into pieces, and serve as a snack, or as an appetizer at an informal supper.

FOCACCIA WITH SAGE

Here, chopped fresh sage is kneaded into the dough, which is shaped to resemble a large leaf.

1 Omit the rosemary and freshly ground black pepper. Finely chop the leaves from 3–5 sprigs of fresh sage.
2 Make the dough, adding the chopped sage to the well in place of the rosemary. Knead the dough, and let rise as directed. Brush a baking sheet with oil.
3 Knock the air out of the dough, and let rest as directed. With a rolling pin and your hands, roll and pull the dough into a 14-inch oval. Transfer to the baking sheet.
4 With a utility knife, make diagonal slashes through the dough to resemble the veins of a leaf, pulling the slits apart with your fingers. Let the dough rise as directed, then brush with 1 tbsp olive oil. Bake as directed.

ANNE SAYS
"If the slashes close while the dough rises, gently open them before baking."

Dimples in dough hold olive oil and rosemary

CHOCOLATE BREAD

🍽 MAKES 1 LARGE LOAF 🍲 WORK TIME 35–40 MINUTES* ♨ BAKING TIME 45–50 MINUTES

EQUIPMENT

heavy-duty electric mixer with paddle and dough hook

1 1/2-quart soufflé dish   bowls

wire rack   dish towels

pastry brush

chef's knife

chopping board

ANNE SAYS
"You'll need a heavy-duty electric mixer to mix and knead dough properly. Use one with paddle and dough hook attachments."

INGREDIENTS

bittersweet chocolate

unsweetened cocoa powder

sugar

unbleached all-purpose flour

unsalted butter

active dry yeast

From the raisins and candied orange peel in panettone it is but a short step to chocolate. So trust an Italian baker to have thought up this delicious dessert bread, darkened with unsweetened cocoa powder and chunks of chopped chocolate. Use good-quality bittersweet chocolate for the best flavor.

GETTING AHEAD
This bread is best the day of baking, but can be tightly wrapped and kept 2–3 days, or it can be frozen.
plus 1 3/4–2 1/4 hours rising time

SHOPPING LIST

2 1/2 tsp	active dry yeast, or 1/2 oz compressed yeast
1 1/2 cups	lukewarm water
1 tbsp	unsalted butter at room temperature, more for bowl and soufflé dish
1/4 cup	unsweetened cocoa powder
4 cups	unbleached all-purpose flour, more if needed
2 tsp	salt
1/3 cup	sugar, more for glaze
4 oz	bittersweet chocolate

ORDER OF WORK

1 MIX, KNEAD, AND LET THE DOUGH RISE; SHAPE THE LOAF

2 BAKE THE LOAF

1 MIX, KNEAD, AND LET THE DOUGH RISE; SHAPE THE LOAF

1 Mix and knead the dough in the heavy-duty electric mixer (see box, page 92).

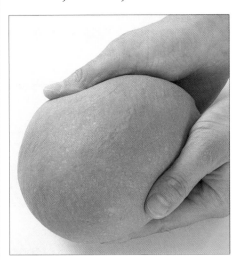

2 Brush a large bowl with melted butter. Put the kneaded dough in the bowl, and flip it so the surface is lightly buttered.

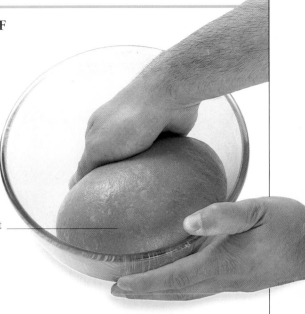

Turn dough against side of bowl for even coating of melted butter

Damp dish towel keeps dough moist as it rises

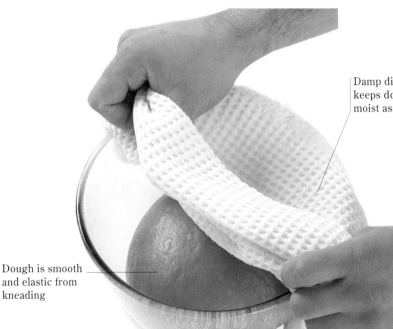

Dough is smooth and elastic from kneading

4 Brush the soufflé dish with melted butter. Set the prepared soufflé dish aside until ready to use.

3 Cover the bowl with a damp dish towel and let the dough rise in a warm place until doubled in bulk, 1–1 1/2 hours.

Chef's knife makes easy work of chopping chocolate

Chunks of chocolate should be coarsely chopped

5 Cut the chocolate into large chunks, then coarsely chop it with the chef's knife. Chill the chocolate.

ANNE SAYS
"Chilling the chocolate a few minutes prevents it from melting when kneaded into the dough."

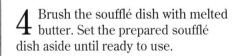

HOW TO MIX AND KNEAD DOUGH IN A HEAVY-DUTY ELECTRIC MIXER

Bread dough is easily mixed and kneaded in a heavy-duty electric mixer. First combine the ingredients using the paddle, then attach the dough hook to knead. This dough-making method can be used in a variety of recipes, using the dry and liquid ingredients as specified.

1 In a small bowl, sprinkle or crumble the yeast over ¼ cup of the water. Let stand until dissolved, stirring once, about 5 minutes.

Paddle attachment combines liquid ingredients, butter, and cocoa evenly

2 Put the dissolved yeast, softened butter, and cocoa powder into the mixer bowl. Pour in the remaining water and mix with the paddle to combine.

ANNE SAYS
"The paddle blends without aerating, producing a smooth batter, the base of an even-textured dough."

Softened butter blends easily

Flour should be completely incorporated before adding more

3 Add half of the flour to the mixer bowl with the salt and sugar, and beat with the paddle just until combined. Add the remaining flour, ½ cup at a time, beating after each addition.

4 Keep adding flour until the dough pulls away from the side of the bowl in a ball. It should be soft and slightly sticky.

5 Attach the dough hook. On medium speed, knead the dough until it is very smooth and elastic, 3–5 minutes. If necessary, add more flour while kneading.

! TAKE CARE !
If the dough climbs up the hook, stop the machine, and push the dough back down.

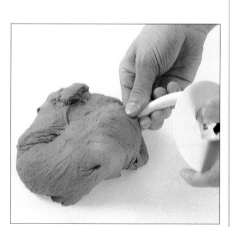

6 Remove the kneaded dough from the dough hook and shape the dough into a ball.

6 Once the dough has risen, turn it from the bowl onto a lightly floured work surface.

7 Knead the dough with your hand just to knock out the air, 15–20 seconds. Cover the dough, and let rest, about 5 minutes.

Dough is spongy in texture after rising

8 Knead the chopped chocolate into the dough until evenly blended, 2–3 minutes. Cover the dough, and let rest, about 5 minutes longer.

ANNE SAYS
"The chocolate is added just before shaping the loaf so it does not inhibit the first rising."

Chocolate is gradually worked into dough

Pinch dough firmly to make tight seam

9 Shape the dough into a loose ball. Fold the sides over to the center, turning and pinching to make a tight round ball.

ANNE SAYS
"For the best flavor, it is important to use good-quality chocolate. A small amount of bittersweet chocolate, with its high proportion of cocoa solids and cocoa butter, goes a long way in baking. Flavor varies from brand to brand, so taste first to find your favorite."

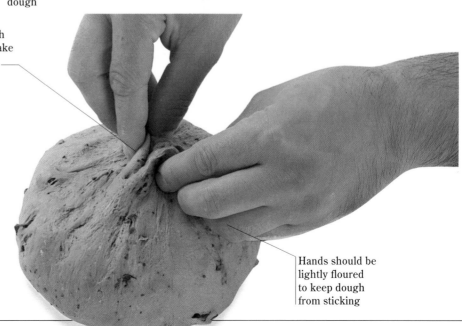

Hands should be lightly floured to keep dough from sticking

10 Carefully put the ball of dough, seam-side down, into the prepared soufflé dish.

Dough will take on shape of soufflé dish as it rises

11 Cover the dish with a dry dish towel, and let the loaf rise in a warm place until the soufflé dish is just full, about 45 minutes.

2 BAKE THE LOAF

1 Heat the oven to 425°F. Brush the top of the loaf with water.

Loaf is brushed with water so sugar sticks and melts while baking

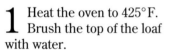

Dough rises to fill soufflé dish

2 Lightly sprinkle the top of the loaf with sugar, spreading it as evenly as possible.

3 Bake the loaf in the heated oven, 20 minutes. Lower the heat to 375°F and continue baking until well browned, 25–30 minutes longer. Remove the bread from the soufflé dish. Turn it over and tap the bottom with your knuckles. The bread should sound hollow, and the sides should feel crisp when pressed.

Tap center of loaf to test if bread is done

Use dish towel to handle hot bread

4 Using a dry dish towel, carefully transfer the bread to the wire rack and let cool completely.

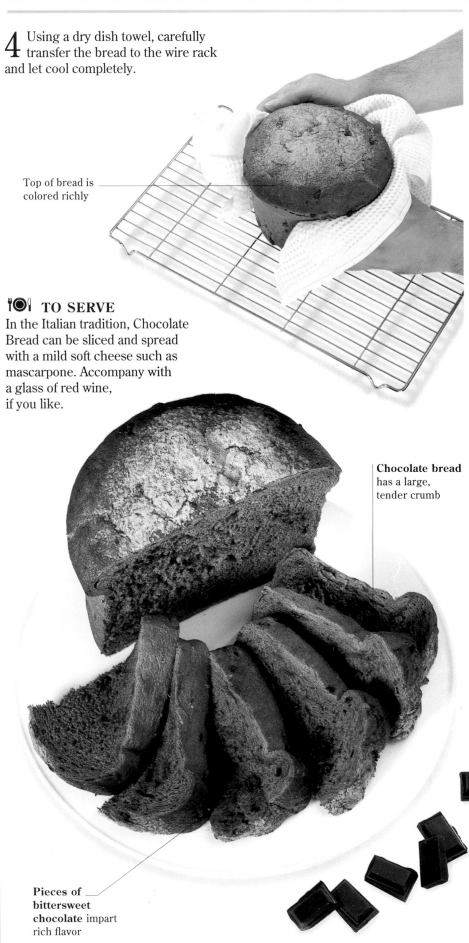

Top of bread is colored richly

🍴 **TO SERVE**
In the Italian tradition, Chocolate Bread can be sliced and spread with a mild soft cheese such as mascarpone. Accompany with a glass of red wine, if you like.

Chocolate bread has a large, tender crumb

Pieces of bittersweet chocolate impart rich flavor

V A R I A T I O N
CHOCOLATE AND ORANGE ROLLS

Here, unsweetened cocoa powder is replaced with grated orange zest and the dough is shaped into large rolls.

1 Omit the cocoa powder. Finely grate the zest of 2 oranges. Make the dough, adding the grated orange zest to the softened butter and liquid ingredients in place of the cocoa powder. Knead the dough, and let rise as directed. Chop and chill the chocolate. Brush 2 baking sheets with melted butter.
2 Knock the air out of the dough and let it rest. Knead in the chocolate and let the dough rest again. Cut the dough in half. Roll 1 piece of dough into a cylinder about 2 inches in diameter. Cut the cylinder into 4 pieces. Shape and divide the remaining dough.
3 Lightly flour the work surface. Cup a piece of dough under the palm of your hand and roll the dough in a circular motion so it forms a smooth ball. Set the ball on 1 of the prepared baking sheets. Shape the remaining dough. Cover with dry dish towels and let the rolls rise in a warm place until doubled in bulk, about 30 minutes.
4 Heat the oven to 425°F. Glaze the rolls as directed, and bake them in the heated oven until they begin to brown, 15 minutes. Lower the heat to 375°F and bake until well browned and the rolls sound hollow when tapped, 15–20 minutes longer. Makes 8 rolls.

AUNT LOUIE'S YULE BREAD

 MAKES 1 LARGE LOAF   WORK TIME 50–55 MINUTES*   BAKING TIME 60–65 MINUTES

EQUIPMENT

9-x5-x3-inch loaf pan

plastic bag

dish towels

strainer

bowls

wire rack

chopping board

rolling pin

metal skewer

pastry brush

chef's knife

saucepan

ANNE SAYS
"You can make and knead the dough in a heavy-duty electric mixer fitted with a dough hook."

As a child, I always looked forward to Christmas and my aunt Louie's Yule Bread. She would bake this spiced fruit bread a month before Christmas so that it had time to moisten and mellow. Then on Christmas Eve we sliced it to eat with a well-aged Stilton cheese.

GETTING AHEAD

Yule bread is delicious the day of baking but can be tightly wrapped and kept in an airtight container for 3–4 weeks. The bread will moisten and the flavor will mellow.

plus 1 3/4–2 1/4 hours rising time

SHOPPING LIST

1 1/2 cups	water
1	English breakfast tea bag
1/2 cup	golden raisins
1/2 cup	dried currants
1/3 cup	candied orange peel
2 1/2 tsp	active dry yeast, or 1/2 oz compressed yeast
2	eggs
4 1/4 cups	unbleached all-purpose flour, more if needed
1/2 tsp	ground cinnamon
1/2 tsp	ground cloves
3 tbsp	granulated sugar
1 tsp	salt
1/2 cup	unsalted butter, softened, more for bowl and loaf pan
2 tbsp	fine brown sugar crystals for glaze

INGREDIENTS

dried currants   English breakfast tea bag

ground cinnamon   ground cloves

active dry yeast   golden raisins

fine brown sugar crystals   candied orange peel

unsalted butter   eggs

unbleached all-purpose flour

granulated sugar

ANNE SAYS
"It is an English tradition to bake this bread with crushed brown sugar crystals on top, but crushed white sugar cubes can be used instead."

ORDER OF WORK

1 MAKE THE DOUGH

2 KNEAD IN THE BUTTER; SHAPE AND BAKE THE LOAF

1 MAKE THE DOUGH

1 Bring 1¼ cups water to a boil. Take from the heat, add the tea bag, and let soak, 5 minutes. Put the raisins and currants in a medium bowl. Discard the tea bag. Pour over the warm tea, and let the fruit soak until plump, 10–15 minutes.

Strain, reserving both fruit and tea

2 Strain the fruit, reserving the tea. Chop the candied orange peel. Set all of the fruit aside.

For best results, water should be 110°–115°F

3 In a small bowl, sprinkle or crumble the yeast over ¼ cup lukewarm water. Let stand until dissolved, stirring once, about 5 minutes.

4 In a small bowl, beat the eggs with a fork just until mixed.

6 Make a well in the center and add the reserved tea, eggs, and dissolved yeast.

Dissolved yeast is smooth and frothy

Deep well holds liquid ingredients

5 Using the strainer, sift the flour, cinnamon, cloves, sugar, and salt into a large bowl.

7 With your fingertips, work the ingredients in the well until thoroughly mixed.

Hand is best tool for mixing dough

8 Gradually draw in the flour and work it into the other ingredients with your hand to form a smooth dough. It should be soft and slightly sticky.

9 Turn the dough onto a floured work surface. Sprinkle the dough and your hands with flour, and begin to knead by holding the dough with one hand and pushing it away from you with the other.

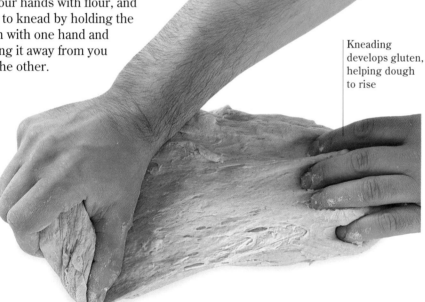

Kneading develops gluten, helping dough to rise

10 Continue to knead by peeling the dough from the surface. Give it a quarter turn and knead until it is very smooth, elastic, and forms a ball, 5–7 minutes. If the dough sticks while kneading, flour the work surface.

11 Wash the large bowl. Brush the bowl with melted butter.

12 Put the kneaded dough in the bowl, and flip it so the surface is lightly buttered. Cover the bowl with a damp dish towel and let the dough rise in a warm place until doubled in bulk, 1–1 1/2 hours.

2 KNEAD IN THE BUTTER; SHAPE AND BAKE THE LOAF

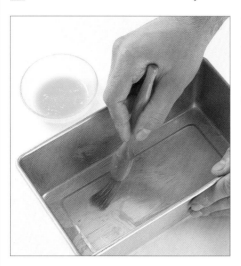

1 Brush the loaf pan with melted butter. Turn the dough onto a lightly floured work surface and knead with your hand just to knock out the air, 15–20 seconds. Cover the dough, and let rest, about 5 minutes.

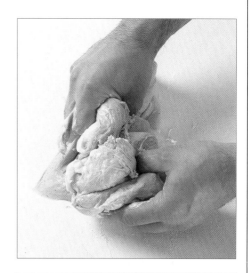

2 Knead in the softened butter, pinching and squeezing the dough with both hands. Knead the dough on the floured work surface until smooth again, 3–5 minutes. Cover, and let rest, 5 minutes longer.

3 Knead the raisins, currants, and candied orange peel into the dough until evenly blended, 2–3 minutes. Cover the dough, and let rest, about 5 minutes.

Knead in fruit by pushing and turning dough

Dough will become smooth with kneading

4 Flour your hands and pat the dough into a 10-x8-inch rectangle on the floured work surface.

5 Starting with a long side, roll the rectangle into a cylinder, pinching and sealing it with your fingers as you go.

ANNE SAYS
"If necessary, flour your hands while rolling dough."

Seam is pinched to form tight cylinder

Dough is colored with spice and tea

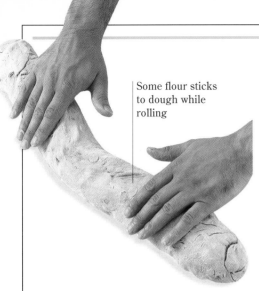

Some flour sticks to dough while rolling

6 With the palms of your hands, roll the cylinder, stretching it until it is about 18 inches long.

7 Working with the cylinder seam-side up, fold the ends over to meet, making it the length of the pan.

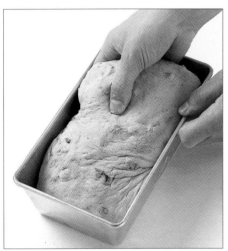

9 Put the sugar crystals in the plastic bag. Crush them with the rolling pin; they should be rather fine.

Rolling pin is ideal tool for crushing sugar

Use strong plastic bag so it does not break

8 Drop the loaf, seam-side down, into the pan. Cover the pan with a dry dish towel, and let the loaf rise in a warm place until the pan is just full, about 45 minutes.

10 Heat the oven to 400°F. Brush the top of the loaf with water.

Loaf is brushed with water so sugar sticks while baking

11 Sprinkle the loaf with the sugar crystals, spreading them as evenly as possible.

Metal skewer
tests if bread is
cooked through

12 Bake the loaf in the heated oven until it rises and begins to brown, about 15 minutes. Lower the heat to 350°F and continue baking until the metal skewer inserted in the center comes out clean, 45–50 minutes longer.

! TAKE CARE !
If the top of the bread browns too quickly, cover it loosely with aluminum foil.

13 Remove the bread from the pan. Turn it over and tap the bottom with your knuckles. The bread should sound hollow and the sides should feel crisp when pressed. Transfer the bread to the wire rack and let cool completely.

⦿ TO SERVE
This bread is a holiday treat. It is good for breakfast, served plain or toasted and spread with butter, or it can be sliced and served with a blue-veined cheese.

Crushed sugar crystals make a crispy glaze

Tea-soaked fruit studs yule bread

VARIATION

YORKSHIRE YULE BREAD
Whiskey-soaked fruit spikes this festive bread.

1 Omit the tea bag and sugar crystals. Soak the raisins and currants in 1/4 cup whiskey, stirring occasionally, 25–30 minutes. Strain the fruit, reserving the whiskey. Chop the candied orange peel and set the fruit aside. Dissolve the yeast as directed.
2 Make the dough, adding the reserved whiskey to the well with the dissolved yeast, eggs, 1 cup lukewarm water. Knead the dough, and let rise as directed.
3 Brush a 1 1/2-quart charlotte mold or soufflé dish with melted butter. Knock the air out of the dough and let rest as directed. Knead in the butter and fruit. Shape the dough into a tight round ball. Put the ball, seam-side down, into the prepared mold. Cover the dough, and let rise as directed.
4 Heat the oven to 400°F. Make the egg glaze: lightly beat 1 egg with 1/2 tsp salt. Brush the loaf with the egg glaze. Using a small strainer, sprinkle the top of the loaf with 1 tbsp confectioners' sugar. If you like, slash a Christmas tree design with a utility knife in the top of the loaf.
5 Bake the loaf, 15 minutes, lower the heat to 350°F, and continue baking, 50–55 minutes longer. Let cool.

OLD-FASHIONED CORNBREAD

🍽️ SERVES 8   🥣 WORK TIME 15–20 MINUTES   ☕ BAKING TIME 20–25 MINUTES

EQUIPMENT

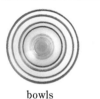
bowls

strainer

pastry brush

chef's knife

chopping board

small saucepan

9-inch ovenproof
cast-iron skillet†

rubber spatula

metal skewer

wire rack

†9-inch round cake pan can also be used

INGREDIENTS

fresh corn

unsalted butter

yellow cornmeal

baking powder

eggs

milk

unbleached
all-purpose flour

sugar

ANNE SAYS
"You can use 1 cup defrosted and drained corn kernels in place of the fresh corn, if you like."

Yellow cornmeal features in this traditional cornbread studded with whole corn kernels and baked in a cast-iron skillet for a deliciously crisp crust. The bread is easily cut into wedges and can be served in or out of the pan.

GETTING AHEAD

The cornbread is best served warm from the oven, but it can be made a day ahead, unmolded, and tightly wrapped. Warm it in the oven before serving.

SHOPPING LIST

2	ears of fresh corn
1/4 cup	unsalted butter, more for skillet and glaze
1 cup	yellow cornmeal
1 cup	unbleached all-purpose flour
1/4 cup	sugar
1 tbsp	baking powder
1 tsp	salt
2	eggs
1 cup	milk

ORDER OF WORK

1 PREPARE THE CORN

2 MAKE THE BATTER AND BAKE THE CORNBREAD

1 PREPARE THE CORN

1 Heat the oven to 425°F. Hold 1 ear vertically and cut from the tip down to the chopping board. Turn the ear and continue cutting, removing as many whole kernels as possible.

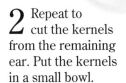

Hold ear firmly against chopping board when removing kernels

2 Repeat to cut the kernels from the remaining ear. Put the kernels in a small bowl.

3 Working over the bowl, use the back of the chef's knife to scrape each ear and remove the corn pulp.

2 MAKE THE BATTER AND BAKE THE CORNBREAD

2 Sift the cornmeal, flour, sugar, baking powder, and salt into a large bowl, and make a well in the center. Add the fresh corn kernels to the well.

1 Brush the skillet with melted butter. Melt the butter for the batter in the small saucepan.

ANNE SAYS

"*Generously buttering the skillet prevents the bread from sticking, and makes the crust crisp and golden.*"

Corn kernels are tender and juicy

Rubber spatula combines ingredients gently

Corn kernels are blended into batter

3 In a medium bowl, whisk the eggs, melted butter, and milk until thoroughly combined.

4 Pour three-quarters of the milk mixture into the well in the flour, and stir with the spatula.

5 Gradually draw in the dry ingredients, adding the remaining milk mixture, and stirring to make a smooth batter.

! TAKE CARE !
Do not overstir the batter or the bread will be heavy.

6 Pour the cornbread batter into the prepared skillet and brush the top generously with melted butter.

Clean skewer means bread is properly baked

Cornbread bakes to a golden brown

7 Bake in the heated oven until the bread starts to shrink from the side of the skillet and the metal skewer inserted in the center comes out clean, 20–25 minutes. Let the cornbread cool slightly on the wire rack.

🍴 TO SERVE
Cut the cornbread into wedges and serve warm. This bread is traditionally served with spicy chili or roasted meats.

VARIATION

CORN MUFFINS WITH ROASTED BELL PEPPER

A sweet bell pepper is roasted to mellow its flavor, then diced and stirred into corn muffin batter. The muffins can be baked in a regular or cast-iron muffin tin.

1 Omit the fresh or frozen corn. Roast, peel, and seed 1 large red bell pepper (see box, right). Cut the pepper halves lengthwise into very thin slices. Cut the slices across into small dice.

2 Heat the oven to 425°F. Generously brush the cups of a 12-cup muffin tin with melted butter; each cup should measure ¼ cup in volume.

3 Make the cornbread batter, using only 1 tbsp sugar and adding the roasted pepper in place of the corn kernels. Spoon the batter into the muffin tin, dividing it equally among the buttered cups. Bake the muffins in the heated oven, until they start to shrink from the sides of the cups and a metal skewer inserted in the center of a muffin comes out clean, 15–20 minutes. Unmold the muffins and let cool slightly. Makes 12 muffins.

ANNE SAYS
"If using a cast-iron muffin tin, make sure it is well seasoned. This helps prevent the muffins from sticking."

HOW TO ROAST, PEEL, AND SEED A BELL PEPPER

Broiling a pepper makes it easy to peel and adds a smoky flavor.

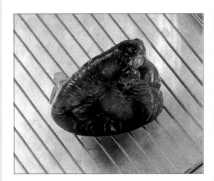

1 Heat the broiler. Set the pepper on the rack about 4 inches from the heat. Broil, turning as needed, until the skin blackens and blisters, 10–12 minutes. Immediately put the pepper in a plastic bag, close it, and let cool.

2 With a small knife, peel off the skin. Rinse the pepper under cold running water and pat dry with paper towels.

3 Cut around the core of the pepper and pull it out. Cut the pepper lengthwise in half and scrape out the seeds. Cut away the white ribs on the inside.

IRISH SODA BREAD

EQUIPMENT

baking sheet

bowls

pastry brush

utility knife†

strainer

I first came across this whole wheat bread in southern Ireland and was surprised by its light, almost cake-like texture. Stone-ground flour makes a great difference to the flavor, and the bread takes very little time to make. Don't confuse it with the version that is a white flour loaf studded with currants.

GETTING AHEAD

Irish Soda Bread is best eaten warm from the oven. Mix the ingredients and bake the bread just before serving.

INGREDIENTS

stone-ground whole wheat flour

buttermilk

butter

baking soda

ANNE SAYS

"Stone-ground wheat flour differs from other wheat flours in that it is ground between stone instead of steel rollers. Stone rollers crush the grain slowly, without stripping away the vitamin-rich wheat germ. Steel rollers crush the grain at a much faster speed, separating the germ and producing a more finely ground flour."

SHOPPING LIST

4 cups	stone-ground whole wheat flour
1 1/2 tsp	baking soda
1 1/2 tsp	salt
2 cups	buttermilk, more if needed
	butter for baking sheet

ORDER OF WORK

1 MAKE THE DOUGH

2 SHAPE AND BAKE THE LOAF

†small knife can also be used

1 MAKE THE DOUGH

1 Heat the oven to 400°F. Using the pastry brush, brush the baking sheet with melted butter.

2 Sift the flour, baking soda, and salt into a large bowl, tipping the bran from the strainer into the bowl.

Stone-ground flour is rich with wheat bran and wheat germ

Sifting aerates flour, catching bran

3 Mix with your hand to combine the dry ingredients, and make a well in the center.

Well holds buttermilk

Large bowl holds ingredients easily

4 In a steady stream, pour the buttermilk into the center of the well.

5 With your hand, quickly draw the flour into the buttermilk to make a soft dough. It should be slightly sticky. Do not overwork the dough or the bread will be heavy. Add a little more buttermilk if the dough seems dry.

2 SHAPE AND BAKE THE LOAF

1 Turn the dough onto a lightly floured work surface, and quickly shape it into a round loaf.

2 Put the loaf on the prepared baking sheet and pat it down with the palms of your hands to form a round, about 2 inches high. With the utility knife, make an "x," 1/2-inch deep, in the top of the loaf.

Deep slashes allow steam to escape during baking

3 Bake the loaf in the heated oven until it is brown, 35–40 minutes. Turn the bread over and tap the bottom with your knuckles. The bread should sound hollow. Transfer the bread to the wire rack and let cool slightly.

🍽️ TO SERVE
Cut the bread into slices or wedges and serve warm, with plenty of butter. Soda bread is a traditional accompaniment to soup or stew, and makes very good toast.

Cross in center of this hearty loaf is traditional decoration

VARIATION
GRIDDLE CAKES

Irish Soda Bread is easily transformed into individual griddle cakes. Cooked on a hot griddle or heavy cast-iron skillet, these cakes are crisp on the outside, moist in the center, and sweetened with a touch of sugar.

1 Heat a griddle or a large cast-iron skillet to medium-low. Make the batter: put 2 cups stone-ground whole wheat flour, 1 1/2 tsp baking soda, and 1 1/2 tsp salt into a large bowl. Stir in 1 cup quick-cooking rolled oats with 3 tbsp brown sugar, and make a well in the center. Pour 2 1/2 cups buttermilk into the well. Stir with a rubber spatula, gradually drawing in the dry ingredients to make a smooth batter.
2 Brush the heated griddle with melted butter. Using a small ladle, drop about 2 tbsp batter onto the hot surface. Repeat to make 5–6 cakes. Cook until the underside of the griddle cakes are golden brown and crisp, about 5 minutes. Turn them over and brown them on the other side, about 5 minutes longer. Transfer to a platter, cover, and keep warm. Continue with the remaining batter, brushing the griddle with more butter as needed. Serve the cakes warm with butter and jam. Makes 20 cakes.

ANNE SAYS
"Seasoning your cast-iron skillet helps prevent foods from sticking. Cover the bottom of the skillet with 1/2 inch of oil and a generous handful of coarse salt, and leave it overnight. Heat it gently on the stove or in the oven until the oil is very hot and almost smoking. Leave the skillet until almost tepid, then discard the oil and salt and wipe the skillet dry. Once a skillet has been seasoned it should never be washed, but wiped out with a cloth while still warm."

VARIATION
SKILLET BREAD

A combination of all-purpose and stone-ground whole wheat flours makes this variation a little lighter than Irish Soda Bread. The dough is cut into wedges and cooked on top of the stove in a heavy cast-iron skillet.

1 Heat a large cast-iron skillet to medium-low. Make the dough: put 3 cups stone-ground whole wheat flour, 1 cup unbleached all-purpose flour, 1 1/2 tsp baking soda, and 1 tsp salt into a large bowl, and make a well in the center. Pour 1 1/2 cups buttermilk into the well. With your hand, quickly draw the flour into the buttermilk to make a soft dough. It should be slightly sticky.
2 Turn the dough onto a lightly floured work surface, and quickly shape it into a round loaf.
3 Pat the dough with the palms of your hands to form a round, about 2 inches high. With a chef's knife, cut the round into 4 wedges.
4 Brush the heated pan with melted butter. Put the dough into the pan, cover, and cook, turning the wedges frequently, until golden brown and puffed, 15–20 minutes. Serve the bread warm, spread with soft cheese or butter. Makes 4 wedges.

SOUTHERN BUTTERMILK BISCUITS

🍴 MAKES 8–10   🥣 WORK TIME 15–20 MINUTES   🍲 BAKING TIME 12–15 MINUTES

EQUIPMENT

2 ³/₄-inch cookie cutter

pastry blender†

bowls

strainer

pastry brush

baking sheet

Homemade biscuits raised with baking powder are standard fare in many Southern homes. Served with country ham, or generous toppings of fresh butter, jam, or honey, they are enjoyed both sweet and savory. This biscuit dough is identical to that of Scottish scones.

GETTING AHEAD
Biscuits take only a few minutes to make, so combine the ingredients and bake them just before serving.

INGREDIENTS

unbleached all-purpose flour

unsalted butter

baking powder

buttermilk

ANNE SAYS
"I enjoy the slightly tangy flavor of buttermilk, but whole milk can also be used."

ORDER OF WORK

1 MAKE THE DOUGH

2 SHAPE AND BAKE THE BISCUITS

SHOPPING LIST

2 cups	unbleached all-purpose flour
2 tsp	baking powder
¹/₂ tsp	salt
¹/₄ cup	unsalted butter, more for baking sheet
³/₄ cup	buttermilk, more if needed

† 2 round-bladed knives can also be used

1 MAKE THE DOUGH

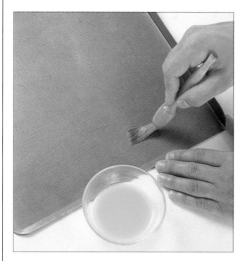

1 Heat the oven to 425°F. With the pastry brush, brush the baking sheet with melted butter.

2 Sift the flour, baking powder, and salt into a medium bowl. Add the butter and cut it into small pieces using the pastry blender or 2 round-bladed knives.

Pastry blender cuts butter into flour without melting it

3 Rub the mixture with your fingertips until it forms fine crumbs, lifting and crumbling to aerate it. Make a well in the center.

4 In a slow, steady stream, pour the buttermilk into the center of the well.

Work quickly so warmth of your hands does not melt butter

5 Quickly toss the flour mixture and buttermilk with a fork to form crumbs.

! TAKE CARE !
Do not overmix the dough or the biscuits will be heavy. Add a little more buttermilk if the crumbs seem dry.

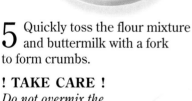
Fork blends dry and liquid ingredients without overmixing

6 Stir the mixture just until the crumbs hold together and form a dough.

2 SHAPE AND BAKE THE BISCUITS

1 Turn the dough onto a floured work surface and knead lightly, 3–5 seconds.

ANNE SAYS

"Don't be tempted to make the dough smooth. The rougher the dough remains, the lighter the biscuits will be."

2 Pat the dough out to a round, 1/2-inch thick. Cut out rounds with the cookie cutter, patting out the trimmings and cutting additional rounds until all the dough has been used.

Cut rounds close together for greatest yield

3 Arrange the biscuits about 2 inches apart on the prepared baking sheet. Bake the biscuits in the heated oven until lightly browned, 12–15 minutes.

⧉ TO SERVE

Pile the biscuits in a basket and serve them hot from the oven with jam and butter.

Jam and butter make these biscuits a breakfast treat

Homemade biscuits are golden on the outside, tender and flaky on the inside

VARIATION
CHIVE DROP BISCUITS

When the quantity of buttermilk is increased, biscuit dough softens and can be dropped from a spoon onto the baking sheet. These made with chives are delicious – ideal for Sunday brunch.

1 Heat the oven to 425°F and brush a baking sheet with melted butter. With a chef's knife, finely chop 1 small bunch of fresh chives.

2 Make the biscuit dough, adding the chives and 1 cup buttermilk to the well. Toss quickly with a fork to form crumbs, then stir the mixture just until it holds together. Do not overmix the dough or the biscuits will be heavy.

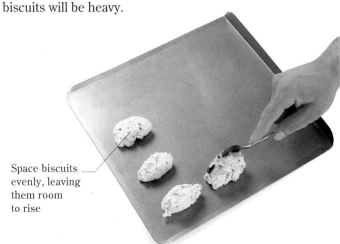

Space biscuits evenly, leaving them room to rise

3 With a tablespoon, drop spoonfuls of dough about 2 inches apart onto the prepared baking sheet. Bake as directed. Makes 10–12 biscuits.

VARIATION
CURRANT SCONES

When studded with dried currants, Southern Buttermilk Biscuits are transformed into this British teatime treat. Serve the scones hot, with butter or clotted cream.

1 Heat the oven to 425°F, and brush a baking sheet with melted butter. Make the glaze: beat 1 egg yolk and 1 tbsp buttermilk until well mixed, and set aside.

2 Sift the flour, baking powder, salt, 1/4 tsp baking soda, and 2 tsp sugar into a medium bowl. Work in the butter as directed, then stir in 2 tbsp dried currants. Finish the dough as directed.

Cut straight down through dough without dragging chef's knife

3 Transfer the dough to a floured work surface. Cut it in half and pat each half into a 6-inch round, about 1/2-inch thick. With a chef's knife, cut each round into 4 wedges. Arrange the wedges about 2 inches apart on the prepared baking sheet. Brush them with the glaze and bake as directed. Makes 8 scones.

ORANGE-ZUCCHINI BREAD

 MAKES 2 MEDIUM LOAVES   WORK TIME 20–25 MINUTES   BAKING TIME 55–60 MINUTES

EQUIPMENT

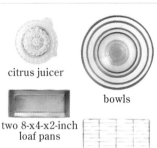
citrus juicer

bowls

two 8-x-4-x-2-inch loaf pans

chef's knife

wire rack

rubber spatula

strainer

grater

metal skewer

pastry brush

chopping board

*Tender vegetables like squash
are often baked in quick breads. Grated zucchini
adds moisture and color to a cinnamon-spiced
batter, with walnuts for hearty crunch.*

GETTING AHEAD
Orange-Zucchini Bread is delicious warm from the oven, but
can be tightly wrapped and kept for 3–4 days. It will moisten
and the flavor will mature. It can also be frozen.

SHOPPING LIST

³/₄ lb	zucchini
1 cup	walnut pieces
2	oranges
3 cups	unbleached all-purpose flour, more for loaf pans
2 tsp	baking powder
2 tsp	ground cinnamon
1 tsp	salt
3	eggs
¹/₂ cup	vegetable oil
1 cup	granulated sugar
¹/₂ cup	light brown sugar
2 tsp	vanilla extract
	butter for loaf pans

INGREDIENTS

zucchini

brown sugar

eggs

oranges

unbleached all-purpose flour

baking powder

ground cinnamon

granulated sugar

walnut pieces

vanilla extract

vegetable oil

ANNE SAYS
*"Be sure to use small, firm
zucchini; large zucchini
contain too much water, and
will make the bread soggy
when baked."*

ORDER OF WORK

1 PREPARE THE
INGREDIENTS

2 MAKE THE BATTER;
BAKE THE BREAD

1 PREPARE THE INGREDIENTS

1 Heat the oven to 350°F. Brush the loaf pans with melted butter. Sprinkle 2–3 tbsp flour in 1 of the pans and turn it to coat the bottom and sides evenly; turn the pan upside down and tap to remove excess flour. Repeat for the second pan.

2 Trim the zucchini and grate them on the coarse grid of the grater; there should be 2 cups grated zucchini.

Keep zucchini at 45° angle for quick grating

3 With the chef's knife, coarsely chop the walnuts. Use your knuckles to guide the knife.

4 Finely grate the zest from the oranges. Halve 1 of the oranges and squeeze the juice; there should be about 1/3 cup.

5 Sift the flour, baking powder, cinnamon, and salt into a large bowl. Mix in the walnuts, and make a well in the center.

2 MAKE THE BATTER; BAKE THE BREAD

1 In a medium bowl, beat the eggs just until mixed. Add the zucchini, orange zest, oil, granulated and brown sugars, vanilla, and orange juice. Stir until thoroughly combined.

Eggs are beaten first so they mix evenly into batter

2 Pour three-quarters of the zucchini mixture into the well in the flour, and stir with the spatula.

Use rubber spatula so ingredients are blended gently

3 Gradually draw in the dry ingredients, adding the remaining zucchini mixture, and stirring to make a smooth batter. Do not overstir the batter or the bread will be heavy.

4 Spoon the batter into the prepared loaf pans, dividing it equally. The pans should be about half full.

5 Bake the loaves in the heated oven until they start to shrink from the sides of the pans and the metal skewer inserted in the center comes out clean, 55–60 minutes. Let the loaves cool slightly, then unmold and transfer to the wire rack to cool completely.

Walnuts add crunch to texture of bread

¶❶¶ TO SERVE
Serve the zucchini bread sliced and spread with cream cheese for a delicious snack. It can also be toasted and buttered for breakfast or tea.

V A R I A T I O N
PUMPKIN BREAD

Canned pumpkin purée makes a good substitute for zucchini. Here, ground nutmeg and cloves are added to spice the batter.

1 Omit the zucchini and oranges. Heat the oven to 350°F, and prepare two 8-x 4-x 2-inch loaf pans as directed.

2 Prepare the batter, using 1 1/2 cups canned pumpkin purée in place of the grated zucchini, and adding 1/2 tsp ground nutmeg and 1/4 tsp ground cloves with the cinnamon.

3 Spoon the batter into the prepared pans and bake until the loaves start to shrink from the sides of the pans and a metal skewer inserted in the center comes out clean, 55–60 minutes. Let cool as directed.

ANNE SAYS
"Fresh pumpkin can also be used. Scrape away the seeds and fibrous threads from a 2-lb piece of pumpkin. Cut the pumpkin skin and flesh into chunks and put them in a large saucepan. Pour in enough water to come one-quarter of the way up the pumpkin, cover, and simmer until the flesh is tender, 25–30 minutes. Drain the pumpkin, scrape the flesh from the skin, and purée it."

V A R I A T I O N
BANANA BREAD

A mash of ripe bananas is delicious baked in quick bread. Spices and nuts add flavor and crunch.

1 Omit the zucchini and oranges. Heat the oven to 350°F. Butter and flour four 5-x 3-x 2-inch loaf pans. Finely grate the zest of 1 lemon.

2 Peel 3 ripe medium bananas and cut them into thirds. In a shallow dish, mash the bananas with a fork to form a smooth paste; there should be 1 1/2 cups mashed banana. Prepare the batter, using the mashed banana in place of the grated zucchini, and adding the lemon zest in place of the orange zest.

3 Spoon the batter into the prepared pans and bake until the loaves start to shrink from the sides of the pans and a metal skewer inserted in the center comes out clean, 35–40 minutes. Let cool as directed.

LEMON-BLUEBERRY MUFFINS

EQUIPMENT

regular
muffin tin

pastry brush   small saucepan

citrus juicer   wire rack

strainer   grater

bowls

rubber spatula

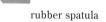
metal skewer

*Grated lemon zest
complements the flavor of
fresh blueberries in these featherweight
muffins. For extra lemon effect, while still hot
from the oven, the muffins are glazed with
lemon juice and sugar.*

GETTING AHEAD
The muffins are best freshly baked and glazed to serve
warm. They can also be frozen.

INGREDIENTS

blueberries   lemon

baking
powder   unsalted butter

vanilla
extract   egg

milk

unbleached
all-purpose flour

sugar

SHOPPING LIST

1/4 cup	unsalted butter, more for muffin tin
2 1/4 cups	unbleached all-purpose flour
1 tbsp	baking powder
1/2 tsp	salt
1/2 cup	sugar
1	lemon
1 1/3 cups	blueberries
1	egg
1 tsp	vanilla extract
1 cup	milk

ORDER OF WORK

1 MAKE THE
MUFFIN BATTER

2 BAKE AND GLAZE
THE MUFFINS

ANNE SAYS
*"I like to use a regular tin
that makes 12 muffins. Each
muffin cup should measure
1/4 cup in volume."*

118

1 MAKE THE MUFFIN BATTER

1 Heat the oven to 425°F. Brush the muffin cups with melted butter. Melt the butter for the batter in the saucepan.

Brush cups with melted butter to prevent muffins from sticking

2 Using the strainer, sift the all-purpose flour, baking powder, and salt into a large bowl.

3 Set 2 tbsp sugar aside for the glaze and stir the remaining sugar into the flour. Make a well in the center.

4 Finely grate the zest from the lemon, leaving the bitter white pith behind.

Lemon zest is yellow part of peel, not bitter white pith

5 Halve the lemon and squeeze the juice. Pick over the blueberries, washing them only if they are dirty.

Blueberries should be plump and sweet

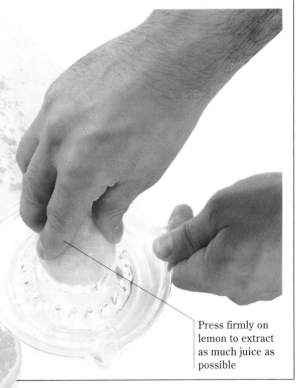

Press firmly on lemon to extract as much juice as possible

6 In a medium bowl, beat the egg just until mixed. Add the melted butter, lemon zest, vanilla, and milk and beat until foamy, about 1 minute.

7 In a slow, steady stream, pour the egg mixture into the well in the flour.

Liquid ingredients are mixed together before being added to well

Gentle folding keeps color of berries from running

9 Gently fold in the blueberries, taking care not to bruise them.

! TAKE CARE !

Mix the batter just until the blueberries are evenly incorporated. Overmixing will toughen the texture of the muffins.

8 Stir with the rubber spatula, gradually drawing in the dry ingredients to make a smooth batter.

Scoop batter and turn bowl to incorporate berries

2 **BAKE AND GLAZE THE MUFFINS**

Muffin cups are filled almost to the top

1 Spoon the batter into the muffin tin, dividing it equally among the buttered cups.

2 Bake the muffins in the heated oven until they start to shrink from the sides of the cups and the metal skewer inserted in the center of a muffin comes out clean, 15–20 minutes. Let the muffins cool slightly on the wire rack.

3 Make the glaze: in a small bowl, stir the reserved sugar with the lemon juice.

Characteristic peak in the middle of muffin develops from high temperature baking

4 Remove the muffins from the tin while they are still warm. Dip the crown of a muffin into the sugar and lemon mixture and set the muffin upright on the wire rack to continue cooling. Repeat with the remaining muffins.

¶○¶ TO SERVE
Serve the glazed muffins while still warm.

Tart lemon glaze complements sweet, plump blueberries

V A R I A T I O N

LEMON-POPPY SEED MUFFINS

Lemon zest and juice are stirred into the batter for these muffins to give more of a lemon flavor, with poppy seeds adding crunch.

1 Omit the blueberries. Heat the oven to 425°F, and brush 9 of the muffin cups with melted butter. Melt the butter for the batter as directed. Grate the zest from the lemon and squeeze the juice.

2 Sift the flour, baking powder, and salt into a large bowl. Stir in all of the sugar. In a medium bowl, beat the egg just until mixed. Add the melted butter, milk, and vanilla, and whisk as directed. Stir in 2 tbsp poppy seeds, then add the lemon zest with the lemon juice. The milk may separate slightly, but this will not affect the finished muffins.

3 Combine the ingredients as directed, and spoon the mixture into the muffin tin, dividing it equally among the buttered cups. Sprinkle the muffins with 2 tsp sugar and bake as directed. Makes 9 muffins.

Breads Know-How

Ingredients

It does not take much to make a loaf of bread. The simplest of loaves are made of flour, yeast, water, and salt. You will find ingredients break down into three main categories: leavening agents, flours, and other ingredients ranging from sugar and spices to buttermilk, cornmeal, and herbs. Remember to use only the best and freshest ingredients available.

Flours

Flour is the foundation of all breads. It can be made from a wide range of finely ground dried grains, seeds, and even roots and tubers, but wheat flour is by far the most common. A wheat kernel has three parts – the bran, the germ, and the endosperm. For white flour, the wheat bran and germ are removed, leaving a refined flour made up of mostly starch and protein. For bread making, the protein content of a flour is the most important characteristic. When dough is kneaded, the string-like proteins in the flour develop gluten, giving the dough its elasticity and structure, a fine mesh in which gas bubbles produced by the yeast are trapped.

The protein content of flour depends on the variety of wheat and the climate in which it is grown. Flour ground from hard-grain wheat has a relatively high protein content and develops strong gluten, while flour ground from softer-grained varieties has more starch and less gluten, desirable for pastries and cakes. All-purpose flour, whether bleached or unbleached, is a combination of hard and soft flours. As flour ages, flavor develops and it makes for better baking. Bleached flour has chemicals added to keep it white and speed aging, while unbleached flour is left to mature naturally. Bread flour has a higher protein content and, as its name implies, is good for bread and pasta. Overall, I prefer using unbleached all-purpose flour for bread and have done so in these recipes. It is widely available, and a bit more versatile than bread flour.

Whole wheat flour is ground from the entire wheat kernel, so it retains all of its natural flavors and nutrients and adds a chewy texture to many breads. Despite the high protein content, whole wheat flour is more difficult to use than all-purpose flour. Because the bran inhibits the effectiveness of the gluten, I often mix the two as in Whole Wheat Bread. Rye flour is ground from the husked rye grain. The flour has little gluten and for a well-risen loaf it must be blended with some all-purpose flour. Other flours, such as buckwheat, are without any gluten at all and must be mixed with generous amounts of wheat flour when yeast is used as the leavening agent.

Leavening Agents

Yeast is the standard leavening agent for bread. It is available dried and fresh or compressed, and is activated when dissolved in a warm liquid, usually water. The yeast transforms the natural sugars in flour into tiny bubbles of carbon dioxide, causing the dough to rise. As dried yeast is universally available, I have suggested its use in this book. Compressed yeast is also easy to find – if you wish to substitute it for dried yeast, use double the weight, and dissolve and mix it in exactly the same way. Fast-acting or rapid-rise yeast is a special variant of dried yeast that raises bread in as little as half the normal time. However, it is mixed quite differently, and should not be substituted directly for dried yeast.

Chemical leaveners such as baking soda and baking powder are also frequently used to leaven bread. They are suited to quick breads with thinner doughs, or batters that lack sufficient gluten to contain the carbon dioxide generated by yeast. Chemical leaveners begin to work as soon as they are mixed with liquid, so these breads should be assembled and baked as quickly as possible.

Other Bread Ingredients

Flour may be the basic ingredient, but many other elements are involved in creating a delicious loaf. Coarse grains, such as cornmeal, bulghur wheat, wheat bran, wheat germ, nuts, and seeds, are often combined with the flour to contribute both texture and flavor. Sweeteners, such as honey, granulated sugar, or brown sugar, help to develop the flavor of a dough or batter. In yeast doughs, sweeteners serve a dual purpose because they also increase the fermentation of the yeast. Salt is indispensable for emphasizing the flavor of plain bread, and dough made without it will have a flat, empty taste.

When fat is added to dough, it softens the texture of the finished loaf and improves its keeping qualities. Butter is a favorite choice, and in some breads, such as Rich Brioche and Kugelhopf with Walnuts, Bacon, and Herbs, it is added in generous quantities. I prefer unsalted butter because its flavor is superior. Vegetable oil is commonly used, and a liberal measure of olive oil contributes moistness as well as flavor in breads like Focaccia with Rosemary. Eggs, particularly egg yolks, add both richness and color to breads, helping them toast well – Challah is an example. Some loaves, such as the French Baguette, contain no fat or egg at all and are best eaten within a few hours of baking.

All of these ingredients must be mixed with liquid to make dough. Water is a neutral choice, while milk softens and whitens the texture of the bread as in Onion and Walnut Crown. Buttermilk gives a subtle tang to yeast as well as quick breads, and fruit juice can add natural sweetness. Tea, potato cooking liquid, and even beer are all possibilities, each contributing a particular quality to the bread.

Any number of fillings, sweet or savory, may be kneaded, rolled, or stirred into a risen dough or batter. During the holiday season I enjoy serving Yorkshire Yule Bread, packed with dried currants, golden raisins, and candied orange peel. Bananas and blueberries impart natural sweetness to quick breads, and in the summer months we bake our surplus garden zucchini into Orange-Zucchini Bread. Sautéed onions, chopped garlic, fresh corn, or a roasted bell pepper are other favorite additions. The flavor of fresh herbs, whether chopped or puréed as in pesto, can permeate an entire loaf of bread, and you will find a variety of cheeses, including Brie, ricotta, mozzarella, and Parmesan, makes its way into the breads in this book.

TECHNIQUES

The bread making process may seem complicated, but in fact the procedure is simple enough. Whether making a yeast-leavened bread or a quick bread, there are a number of techniques on which you can rely.

YEAST BREADS

Once you have mastered a few basic techniques for making yeast breads, you can apply them to virtually every loaf you bake. You will learn how to dissolve yeast in just the right temperature of water so it grows and works to full advantage. You will see how to make dough both in a bowl and directly on a work surface. Usually the dough is completed in one sequence, but in Split-Top White Bread, as a preliminary step, the dissolved yeast is mixed with a little flour to make a sponge, improving the flavor and texture of the bread. I will also show you how to knead dough, as well as how to let it rise.

When making yeast dough, I never give an exact quantity of flour because the amount can vary significantly. Not only does flour differ from mill to mill and brand to brand, but it also changes with age and humidity of storage. Therefore, I advise adding flour gradually to dough, stirring after each addition. The dough is ready to knead when it is soft and slightly sticky – more flour will be worked in during the kneading process. Note also that yeast feeds on sugar, so it will work faster when in contact with sweet ingredients. Salt, however, slows its growth, so is always mixed with other ingredients – never let salt come in direct contact with the yeast itself.

Kneading is the most important technique when making a yeast-leavened loaf, because it develops the elasticity of the dough. It also creates the structure that holds the gases produced by the yeast and supports the dough as it rises. You will need a forceful hand to push and turn a firm dough on the work surface until it is smooth and elastic. With softer doughs, such as Small Brioches and Focaccia with Rosemary, slapping and throwing is more effective.

Rising is the next step in the process of making yeast bread. Dough should be left to rise, or proof, in a warm, humid, draft-free place. The optimum temperature is around 85° F. I often leave dough to rise in the oven heated just by the gas pilot. For an electric oven, heat the oven for about 10 seconds and switch it off. The top of a warm radiator or a rack set over a gently steaming pan on the stove are other alternatives, but be sure the bowl does not get too hot. Dough can also be left to rise in the refrigerator for convenience. The cold will slow down the activity of the yeast, so rising may take 5 hours or overnight. Be sure the top of the bowl is covered with a damp cloth or a tight seal of plastic wrap to keep the dough moist. Likewise, once shaped, some doughs can be left to rise in the refrigerator overnight. Let them come to room temperature before baking. Small rolls can be shaped and frozen up to 1 month. Let them thaw before baking.

Knowing when dough has risen sufficiently and the gluten has stretched to maximum capacity is key to a successful loaf. In general, dough should double in bulk, and when you press a finger deep into the dough the mark will remain – if the dough springs back, it is not ready. You will see what to look for and how to test the dough in detailed "how-to" boxes.

A loaf of bread is recognizable by its shape. You will learn how to roll dough for French Baguette into long sticks, how to make Small Brioches so their "heads" do not slip to the side during baking, and how to twist egg-enriched dough into a variety of ornamental rolls. Rustic loaves of Sourdough Bread are left to rise in cloth-lined bowls so the soft dough holds its shape. Focaccia with Sage is slit into a distinctive leaf shape, Challah is braided into a characteristic tress.

Just before baking, the top of a loaf is often

glazed and sometimes slashed. You will learn how to glaze doughs so the finished loaves are shiny or golden, soft or crisp as the case may be. Slashing allows the dough to expand in a neat design without cracking – the deeper the cuts, the more the bread will open to reveal the crumb. I will show you a variety of methods, some practical, like the diagonal slashes made to release steam as Seeded Rye Bread bakes, and some decorative, such as the hedgehog finish given to Orange Juice Breakfast Bread.

QUICK BREADS

As their name implies, quick breads are a complete contrast to yeast-leavened breads. These recipes can and should be made in just a few minutes, and include muffins and biscuits as well as larger loaves with a characteristic soft, crumbly texture, such as Orange-Zucchini Bread and Old-Fashioned Cornbread. You will see how to combine the wet and dry ingredients to make a dough that is sticky and rough in appearance – sometimes it is thin enough to be a pourable batter. In complete contrast to yeast bread techniques, quick and gentle mixing is vital so elasticity is not developed in the flour, and the finished bread remains light and airy.

As with other volumes in the *Look & Cook* series, I have also included techniques for the other ingredients that are used in these bread recipes. For instance, you will find out how to chop herbs, how to roast, peel, and seed a bell pepper, and how to peel, seed, and chop tomatoes.

CHOOSING BREADS

You will find there is a bread to accompany almost every meal. When choosing a recipe, think about the whole menu, its flavor and feel. For casual suppers of soups and stews, serve crusty loaves like Wheat Ear Baguette, Sourdough Bread, or quick and easy Irish Soda Bread if you're short of time. Southern

Buttermilk Biscuits are delicious with a traditional bacon and egg breakfast, and make great lunchtime sandwiches of baked ham and honey mustard.

For formal dinners, delicate Dinner Rolls served warm with a pat of butter are in order. And for a very special breakfast in bed, Chocolate and Orange Rolls served with mascarpone cheese, fresh fruit, and steaming coffee are the ultimate indulgence.

Pizza and stuffed breads make fine lunch and dinner fare. Just add a crispy green salad, and Chicago Deep-Dish Pizza with its flavorful and hearty topping is perfect for a relaxed evening meal. Try Pesto Garland Bread with simply prepared pasta. Serve Spiced Lamb Pies for lunch with a yogurt and cucumber salad. Easy!

STORING BREADS

All yeast breads are best eaten the day of baking, and some, like Potato-Chive Monkey Bread and Focaccia with Rosemary, are particularly good still warm. Cornmeal Pizzas with Onion Confit and Gorgonzola, of course, should be eaten hot from the oven. Nonetheless, many breads can be stored up to 2 days, and some even longer if they contain a high proportion of fat. However, French Baguette, which has no fat at all, is stale within a few hours. Once the loaves are thoroughly cool, wrap them tightly in plastic wrap or aluminum foil. If stored in the refrigerator, loaves will last longer, and if frozen they can usually be kept for several months.

Storage time for quick breads depends very much on their richness: plain breads like Southern Buttermilk Biscuits and Currant Scones are best eaten at once, while still warm. However, breads with good quantities of eggs, sugar, and, most importantly, fat, fruit, or nuts, can be kept in an airtight container for 1 week or more. Banana Bread is a good example.

To restore freshness to day-old yeast bread, wrap it loosely in a brown paper bag and put it in a warm oven until heated through, 5–10 minutes. Do not throw stale bread away, but grind it into fresh breadcrumbs in a food processor or blender, or slice or cut it into cubes to make golden croûtons.

BREADS AND YOUR HEALTH

Complex carbohydrates are being emphasized as an integral part of a healthful diet, so we are encouraged to eat a variety of whole grains, pasta, and breads. In addition to being sources of energy, they provide vitamins, minerals, and fiber as well.

In bread making, as in all other kinds of cooking, it is important to start with the best and freshest ingredients possible. In many parts of the country, you can find organic flours, some locally milled. For flavor and freshness, the availability of these flours is worth investigating. Check your health or whole food store.

In a strict sense, the simpler the bread the better it is for you. Obviously, breads made without added fat are the best of all. It is important to note, however, that once spread with butter and jam, even the simplest bread loses some of its virtue. Good bread has plenty of flavor and is quite delicious served unadorned. French Baguette and Sourdough Bread are two famous examples.

Most breads do contain some fat – a little milk, olive oil, or vegetable oil. Pita, Sesame Breadsticks, and Irish Soda Bread fall into this category, while others are made with quite a lot of butter and eggs – Small Brioches, Kugelhopf with Walnuts, Bacon, and Herbs, and Yorkshire Yule Bread to name a few. There is plenty of room for all of these breads in a healthful diet. Choose them wisely. Moderation, as always, is key.

Remember that we do not live by bread alone. Bread and its dietary value do not stand in isolation. Consider the meal as a whole. Seek balance – enjoy fruits, vegetables, proteins, and bread.

HOW-TO BOXES

In each of the recipes in **Classic Breads** *you will find pictures of all the techniques used. However, some basic preparations appear in a number of recipes and these are shown in extra detail in these special "how-to" boxes:*

MICROWAVE

When making bread, the microwave can be helpful in preparing certain basic ingredients. You can melt butter, as well as heat milk and water. Be sure to follow the manufacturer's instructions for cooking speeds and times.

For yeast breads, the microwave is sometimes used to speed the rising process, but recipes need to be adapted for its use. The breads in this volume have been developed using traditional techniques, and are best suited to the bread-making methods specified in each recipe.

INDEX

ACKNOWLEDGMENTS

Photographers' Assistants Nick Allen and Sid Sideris

Chef Eric Treuille
Home Economist Maddalena Bastianelli

US Editors Julee Binder and Constance Mersel

Typesetting Rowena Feeny and Axis Design

Text film by Disc to Print (UK) Limited

Production Consultant Lorraine Baird

*Anne Willan would like to thank her chief editor
Jacqueline Bobrow and associate editor Valerie Cipollone
for their vital help with writing this book and researching
and testing the recipes, aided by Karen Ryan and
La Varenne's chefs and trainees.*

WEIGHTS AND MEASURES

MEASUREMENT CONVERSIONS

US Cups	Metric
1 tbsp	15 ml
$^1/_8$ cup	30 ml
$^1/_4$ cup	60 ml
$^3/_8$ cup	90 ml
$^1/_2$ cup	125 ml
$^2/_3$ cup	150 ml
$^3/_4$ cup	175 ml
1 cup ($^1/_2$ pint)	250 ml
1 $^1/_4$ cups	300 ml
1 $^1/_2$ cups	375 ml
2 cups (1 pint)	500 ml
2 $^1/_2$ cups	600 ml
3 $^3/_4$ cups	900 ml
1 qt (4 cups)	1 litre
1 $^1/_4$ quarts	1.25 litres
3 US pints	1.5 litres
2 quarts	2 litres

Standards
1 tsp = 5 ml
1 tbsp = 15 ml
1 fl oz = 30 ml
1 ml = 0.035 fl oz
1 UK pint = 20 fl oz
1 US pint = 16 fl oz
1 litre = 33 fl oz
          (1 US qt)

Length Conversions
1 cm = 0.3 in

SOLID WEIGHT CONVERSIONS

US	Metric
$^1/_2$ oz	15 g
1 oz	30 g
2 oz	60 g
3 oz	90 g
4 oz ($^1/_4$ lb)	120 g
5 oz	150 g
6 oz	180 g
8 oz ($^1/_2$ lb)	240 g
12 oz ($^3/_4$ lb)	360 g
1 lb (16 oz)	480 g

Standards
1 oz = 30 g   1 lb = 16 oz (480 g)
1 g = 0.35 oz   1 kg = 2.2 lb

OVEN TEMPERATURE CONVERSIONS

°F	Gas	°C
225	$^1/_4$	110
250	$^1/_2$	120
275	1	140
300	2	150
325	3	160
350	4	175
375	5	190
400	6	200
425	7	220
450	8	230
475	9	240
500	10	260